D0907417

RUM ROW

DISCARDED

Flat Hammock Press
5 Church Street
Mystic, CT 06355
(860) 572-2722
www.flathammockpress.com

Rum Row originally published 1959
© 2007 by Flat Hammock Press

All rights reserved. No part of this book may be reproduced or transmitted
in any form without written consent of the publisher.

Printed in the United States of America

10 9 8 7 6 5 4 3 2 1

Library of Congress Cataloging-in-Publication Data

Carse, Robert, 1902-1971.
  Rum row: the liquor fleet that fueled the Roaring Twenties / Robert Carse.
      p. cm.
  Originally published: New York: Rinehart, 1959.
  ISBN 0-9758699-4-9
  1. Prohibition—United States. 2. Smuggling—United States.
  HV5089.C27 2006
  364.1'33--dc22

                                        2006010156

ISBN10: 0-9758699-4-9
ISBN13: 978-0-9758699-4-9

RUM ROW

THE LIQUOR FLEET THAT FUELED THE ROARING TWENTIES

by Robert Carse

FLAT HAMMOCK PRESS
MYSTIC, CONNECTICUT

Robert Carse was the author of nearly 50 books, including:

A Cold Corner of Hell
Dunkirk, 1940
Towline
Early American Boats
Ports of Call
The Young Mariners
The Young Colonials
Fire in the Night
The Long Haul
The Twilight of Sailing Ships
Your Place in the Merchant Marine
Great American Harbors
The Seafarers
The Moonrakers
The Rivermen
The Age of Piracy
Blockade
The Unconqurered
There Go the Ships
Lifeline
Horizon
Siren Song
Heart's Desire
Pacific
Deep Six
Rum Row
The High Country
From the Sea And the Jungle
Great Circle
Great Venture
The Winner
Hilton Head Island in the Civil War
A Book of Smugglers
Go Away Home
Ocean Challenge
The Castaways
Hudson River Hayride
Glory Haul
The Fabulous Buccaneer
The Beckoning Waters
Keepers of the Lights

CONTENTS

"So far as the record goes, no lover of drinking has yet gone out into the night and shot himself as a gesture of protest."

Gilbert Seldes, *The Future of Drinking*, 1930

FOREWORD

The account told here does not present the full history of Rum Row or of Prohibition. Such a work is impossible. The source material is too fragmentary, and far too many people who have participated in the activities of those days are unwilling to have their names in print, for manifest reasons. In addition, a great deal of the record was never written and has become obscurely mixed with folklore. Wherever possible, of course, I have done my utmost to give the story in confirmed detail.

Deep gratitude is expressed to Commodore John S. Baylis, USCG, Ret., who not only was vigorous in his pursuit and capture of rum runners, but had the acumen during his years of Rum Row service to gather and retain a mass of information and a photographic collection which the Coast Guard cannot match and which are his treasured personal property. When starting this book, in fact, I was advised by the Coast Guard to seek out the commodore as my best available source.

Others who have been of distinct aid to me are Commander C. R. Peele, USCG, Ret., and Lieutenant Commander E.V. Wyatt, USCG, Ret., both veterans of the Rum Row patrol and men with keen and trustworthy memories. Then there are Lieutenant R.H. Scarborough, USCG, Public Information Officer by direction of the Commander, Third Coast Guard District; Mr. F. Langton Corwin, editor and publisher of *The Suffolk Times*, Greenport, New York; Mr. William Sandwald, of Shelter Island, New York; and the necessarily nameless.

R.C.

Book One

THE GOLDEN YEARS

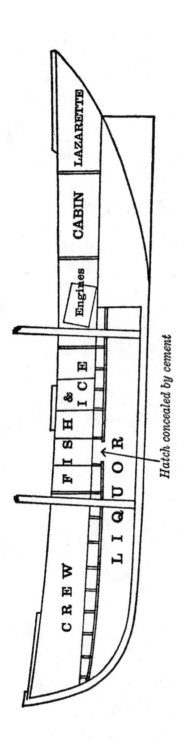

CREW   LIQUOR   FISH & ICE   Engines   CABIN   LAZARETTE

Hatch concealed by cement

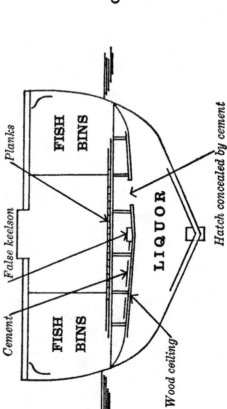

Cement   False keelson   Planks

FISH BINS   FISH BINS

LIQUOR

Wood ceiling

Hatch concealed by cement

SKETCH

of

Am. Fisherman "Marianne",
Seized at New London, Ct.,
by

COAST GUARD SECTION BASE FOUR

April 11, 1930.

Showing false bottom,
false keel, concealed
hatch and hold where
large liquor cargo was
stored.

CHAPTER ONE

It was in the great American tradition. Now that the issue was decided and the Eighteenth Amendment was part of national law, the public lost interest in Prohibition. The drinkers believed that, somehow, they would go on drinking. Members of the various Dry groups which had pressed for the legislation were convinced that all manufacture of alcohol for human consumption, and also any attempts at illicit sale, could be stopped rather easily.

Midnight, January 16, 1920, when Prohibition went into effect, passed almost unnoticed. Some few New York City hotels set their tables with black cloths as a gesture of mourning, and yet throughout the country there was nothing like a formal ceremony. Prohibition had been ratified by the legislatures of forty-six states, and forty-three had created enforcement codes of their own to implement the action of the Federal government. Congress had given a two-thirds vote for passage over President Wilson's veto. The work of the Women's Christian Temperance Union, which had lasted for four decades, had come to a successful end. Mrs. Ella A. Boole, the head of the organization, and her cohorts no longer had to ask the question, "Can you change the mind of your dripping Wet Senator?" (The W.C.T.U. answer to this was, "No, but you can change your Senator.")

But a conservative estimate of the distillery and brewery business at the time of enactment was set at more than a billion dollars. The national convention of the American Federation of Labor at Atlantic City in June, 1919, had been very critical of World War I liquor restrictions, asked for a modification of the proposed Volstead Act and adopted the slogan, "No Beer, No Work." Following the convention, members of the A.F.L. demonstrated outside the Capitol in Washington and made known their desires.

Among the big distillers and liquor wholesalers were men who recognized that they had been tardy in their opposition to the new law. For too long they had derided the Women's Christian Temperance Union because of oaths such as the following: signed and then recited by junior converts:

> I promise not to buy, sell or give
> Alcoholic liquors while I live;
> From all tobacco I'll abstain
> And never take God's name in vain.

The artistic merits and the prophetic powers of Professor J.G. Dailey of Philadelphia, Pennsylvania had been underestimated by the liquor interests. The professor had written, in 1911, a song for the W.C.T.U. which Mrs. Boole described as "dignified but catchy music." The title for the piece was "A Saloonless Nation in 1920," and it had been fervently sung at all public meetings, local, state and national, held by the temperance organization. Only a small number of the distillers had sensed Professor Dailey's foresight and moved out large stocks of bourbon and rye whiskey to warehouses at Nassau in the Bahamas.

Despite these earlier withdrawals, when the law came into effect, distilleries were shut down with immense amounts of liquor in stock; the breweries were full; and a great amount of industrial alcohol produced for World War I purposes was still on hand. Mrs. Boole and the other Dry leaders watched keenly for the first legal enforcement. January 28, 1920, twelve days after the law became effective, a search was made in New York City. It was suspected by agents of the Internal Revenue Department that some one-gallon stills of the compact do-it-yourself type were being used. But none was found.

Then, on February nineteenth, a pair of Department agents assigned to Prohibition work were arrested in Baltimore, Maryland, on corruption charges. The drinking public had already begun to spend money for illicit liquor, and this spread forth inevitably into graft. Within less than a year—by December, 1921—there were one hundred agents in New York City alone who were discharged from their service because of corruption.

The nation was in no wise dry. Five major sources of illicit liquor satisfied the popular demand: medicinal, sold by doctors' prescriptions and through drugstores; "near beer" that was often given a strengthening squirt of alcohol just before it was sold over a speakeasy bar; industrial alcohol from existing stocks; still-made alcohol and its less potent cousins, home-brew beer and home-pressed wine; and smuggled liquor from the Bahamas, Bermuda, Canada, Mexico, Cuba and Europe.

Smuggled liquor, always described when sold as being "right off the boat," was accepted as the best and drew the highest prices. Government enforcement authorities were forced to admit that the Atlantic, Gulf and Pacific coastlines stretched for 12,000 miles. The northern and southern borders extended 3,700 miles and the Great Lakes and adjacent river frontage took in another 3,000. But to cover this enormous complex was a force of only 1,550 prohibition agents, 3,000 customs agents and a Coast Guard complement of approximately 11,000 men.

The national borders, and in particular the Atlantic coast, were vulnerable to most any form of liquor-smuggling operation. The thirsty from Maine to Florida were willing to pay for what they wanted as long as it looked and smelled and had anything like the effect of a pre-Prohibition drink. There were men ready to satisfy their demands. Smuggling, like the consumption of alcohol, was an old American custom.

CHAPTER TWO

Captain William McCoy, later to be known along Rum Row as "the McCoy" or "the real McCoy" because of the excellence of the liquor he sold and his fair prices, was among the very first to become a seagoing smuggler. He was attracted to the trade for various reasons, one of them being that he was poor and quite eager to make some money. But he also had a vast, lasting love of the sea; he delighted in handling vessels under sail; and the risks involved, although he probably was never conscious of the fact, appealed to his sense of adventure.

He was a big man, six feet two, broad through the shoulders, narrow in the hips, and powerful. Like many other lifetime sailors, he was born inland, at Seneca Falls, New York, but moved early with his family to Philadelphia. His father was a bricklayer and young McCoy worked as his apprentice. Then one day he went down to the waterfront and saw at anchor in the Delaware River the Pennsylvania state training ship *Saratoga*. He stood a long time looking at her tall masts and the sweep of her yards, the grace of bowsprit, bow, hull. Back home his father was told to get another apprentice; he, Bill, was going to be a sailor. There was no firm objection to his ambition, however. His father had served in the United States Navy as a young man, during the Civil War; he had been aboard the USS *Powhattan*, the *Moccasin* and the *Gloucester* on North Atlantic Squadron blockade duty.

McCoy spent two years as a cadet on the *Saratoga*, graduated first in his class and received his third mate's license. But advancement was slow in the merchant service. He spent his twenties, some of his best years, aboard a succession of yachts and coastwise steamers, and was not particularly content with the chief mate's job aboard the *Olivette* at seventy-five dollars a month on the Havana-Key West run when, in 1900, his family moved to Florida.

His brother Ben, with their father to help him, started a boatyard in Jacksonville. Bill McCoy gave up his job as mate and joined them. The yard thrived; they were good builders and sent fine boats off the ways. Boats bearing their name plates were bought by the Vanderbilts, John Wanamaker, Maxine Elliott and Andrew Carnegie. With prosperity, the brothers expanded. They established a motor-boat service that used the inside passage from Jacksonville to Palm Beach, and ran from Palm Beach to Fort Meyers through the ever-glades. Then bus lines began competition, took away their trade. Bill McCoy was nearly broke and close to middle age when Prohibition became law.

He was tempted to leave the beach by an older fisherman friend who called upon him one day in early 1920. The fisherman, hither-to notorious for his poverty, was wearing the more garish kind of Palm Beach specialty-shop clothes, smoking a dollar cigar and driv-ing a long and very high-priced roadster. Would McCoy, he asked calmly, like to make a hundred dollars a day?

McCoy got over shock, then listened and considered. His newly ornate friend had a proposition to offer. Men who could handle a schooner under sail were few along the Florida east coast, and there was a seventy-footer named the *Dorothy W.* which could carry a cargo of rye whiskey from Nassau to Atlantic City. While master of her, McCoy would receive the aforementioned sum of one hundred dollars daily. McCoy went to look at her and was dis-appointed. She was old, a drab and weary craft, perhaps not even seaworthy. He turned down her command and still tried to keep the family motorboat service in operation.

There was, though, a dramatic sense in his nature, and he began to liken himself to John Hancock. He remembered that what was popularly believed to be an unjust law had been passed in Hancock's time. Hancock had defied it, run in contraband despite it and later had been respected to such a degree that he was made Governor of Massachusetts. But more important than the historical precedent was the urge to get back to sea and make a profitable living.

McCoy sold the motorboats with the consent of his brother Ben, took the money north and looked for a vessel that would be suitable as a rum-runner. He found her in August 1920 in Gloucester, Massachusetts. She was the schooner *Henry L. Marshall*, ninety feet long, of white pine construction and designed for the fishing trade, built in the James yard in Essex, Massachusetts. She carried pole masts and had a semi-knockabout rig, twin propellers and a motor that made a speed of seven knots. McCoy closely inspected her hold space and calculated that she would take fifteen hundred cases of liquor in the usual cumbersome distillers' boxes, but if stowed differently, three thousand cases in burlap-covered lots of six bottles each, at double the profit for a voyage.

He bought the *Marshall* for sixteen thousand dollars, then spent another four thousand dollars to have her refitted. While the refit was being done in Gloucester, he stayed with her to check the work. He was at the seaward side of the yard dock one dusk when he saw the *Arethusa*.

The lovely, black-hulled, two-masted schooner was entering from offshore with the last of the day's radiance upon her. She rounded Eastern Point, slipped past Norman's Woe, and her sails shone and the foam thrust from her forefoot glimmered and the wake she left was a golden path. McCoy watched her until she had gone alongside the dock, her lines were secured and her canvas furled. That ship he would own, he promised himself; none other that he had ever seen had so caught his fancy. But she belonged to the East Coast Fisheries Company, and he lacked the money for her, must sail the *Marshall* until he made it.

McCoy mustered a crew of fishermen from the Gloucester beach who had no particular respect for the Eighteenth Amendment. Then he loaded stores and water aboard and set the *Marshall* on her course for Nassau. The Bahamian port was the best place for him to pick up cargo in his new trade.

Nassau, he discovered as he ran into the harbor and went ashore, was no longer slumberous without her winter tourist crowds. A stir of excitement rippled along Bay Street. The barmen at the Colonial Hotel, the Royal Victoria, the Lucerne, the Atlas had more to do than slap at flies and swab mahogany during the heat-heavy hours of afternoon. Americans with large amount of cash were in town. There were not many of them yet, but they spent ardently, preferred neat rye or bourbon whiskey to any sort of rum swizzle. They talked in broad, bright terms of the liquor stocks they would buy wholesale here and ship out to be smuggled into the States.

A smart young pair of brothers, local men named MacPherson, had already started business in competition with the Americans. The MacPhersons had imported one thousand cases of Scotch whiskey to be sent north to the American market. Staid circles close to Government House were shocked; it was remembered that Nassau had suffered a very bad name in colonial days as a pirate base, and in the Civil War had attracted another raffish aggregation from the blockade-runner crews. The MacPherson enterprise was described as scandalous until the brothers pointed out that for every case of whiskey that cleared port, the Bahamian government received six dollars in revenue.

McCoy was claimed immediately by one of the American whole-sale liquor buyers. He was Bill Hain, an old friend. Hain had been keeping a vigil upon the harbor from a waterfront bar. He had seen the *Marshall* come in and moor, then recognized McCoy, and rushed to meet him before he was lost to some other speculator eager to pick up a vessel for charter.

Hain discussed the details of the deal with McCoy right on Bay Street. He pointed to the donkey-drawn drays that at his order were being pulled alongside the *Marshall*. He wanted to know, how about fifteen hundred cases, McCoy was to be paid ten dollars a case for delivery?

McCoy asked where delivery was to be made. He was told, in St. Catherine's Sound, on the Georgia coast below Savannah. Launches had been engaged to take off such cargo and bring it ashore. McCoy was then interested in the expected date of cargo delivery. Hain said that it would be as soon as McCoy could arrive with the schooner.

McCoy glanced around at the *Marshall*. He was not a drinking man, but he knew that his crew were, and they had not yet been ashore. They stood on the schooner's deck and looked with disfavor at the signs of loading and quick departure. He mentioned crew morale to Hain.

Hain said that he would take care of that. He swept his arm

above his head, and out of the patches of shadow on Bay Street slant-wheeled hacks appeared. Whips snapped and the drivers advanced their horses from a dozing walk into a trot. Then Hain talked to the crew of the *Marshall*, invited them to be his guests. They jumped into the hacks, and Hain called from the seat of the first, "Grant's Town!"

McCoy had visited Grant's Town in the past to collect crews. It was "over the hill" from Nassau proper, and inhabited by Negroes, who lived in gray, shambling wooden houses. A section of it maintained bars; rum was cheap; there were pretty mulatto girls and player pianos. Hain had a good understanding of crew morale.

Meanwhile, McCoy went aboard the *Marshall* to superintend the loading. The drays bore twenty-five cases apiece. Each case was made up of what the native tally clerk told him were locally called "hams" of six bottles each. It was the same economical method of stowage that McCoy had calculated in Gloucester. The bottles were packed in their straw wrappers in a pyramidal form—three, then two, then one—and then sewed tightly inside burlap with doubled sail twine. They took up half the space of the original cases, weighed much less, were a great deal easier to stow and would take a lot more rough treatment.

But in the space of an hour Hain was back with the crew. The men loped onion-eyed drunk and extraordinarily happy out of the hacks, and somehow managed to get aboard. McCoy finished the loading, secured for sea and made the final arrangements with Hain. Hain was leaving Nassau at once by seaplane for the States. He would meet the schooner in St. Catherine's Sound.

Longshoremen who had done the loading cast off the mooring lines for McCoy. The crew sat numb, drowsy after the delights of Grant's Town. But McCoy managed to pull away from the dock with the help of the motor, headed the schooner for the harbor entrance. Then, the trade wind full in their faces, some of the sailors staggered to their feet and gave him a hand in raising sail.

He was keenly impatient to set his course for the mainland, but he realized that when he approached it, he would risk arrest and the confiscation of his vessel. So he sailed first for the small Bahamian port of West End, put in and procured from the authorities there a second set of clearance papers. Those issued him at

West End stated that he sailed bound for Savannah "in ballast." They might help if he were captured on the American coast.

The crew sobered swiftly at sea, stood their watches in good style, and McCoy brought the schooner in across the Gulf Stream sweep, took bearings and then trimmed canvas and pointed through the surf into the inlet chosen by Hain. The ship had been at sea for three days of fair weather. Now the wind lifted to gale force and in the shallow inlet waters a rough, dangerous chop was running.

Hain was there, in the darkness and the wind, and with him the launches from shore to receive the cargo. Sailors bent on their knees on the *Marshall's* heaving deck and passed burlap-covered packages from hand to hand and to the launch crew without breakage. Then, just before dawn, a plane was heard. They caught sight of it as it circled low to land; it was a seaplane with government markings on the wings. Hain cursed and gave a harsh order; one hundred cases went over the side.

But the plane was not out to capture rum-runners. Its pilot did not even come near the schooner. Hain paid off McCoy and they shook hands and parted. McCoy set a jib, eased ahead and brought his anchor aboard, steered into the morning sun for the open sea. He was back in Nassau a week after he had left, with fifteen thousand dollars in cash locked in a drawer in the cabin. If work like this kept up, he told himself, he would soon be able to buy his black-hulled sweetheart, the *Arethusa.*

Sitting in the quiet of his furnished room at Mrs. Kemp's while he gazed out at the *Marshall* at anchor in the Nassau harbor, McCoy began to doubt his good fortune, however, and was given to skeptical thought about the future. It seemed that such a bonanza could not last. There must be a rough side to it. Still, Bill Hain was in port again and had offered him another run. Hain talked with iridescent enthusiasm.

The American liquor market was expanding all the time, he said. Stateside, the drinking public was already wary of the effects of partially converted industrial alcohol, which, when mixed with most anything brown and some tap water, was sold as whiskey. Men had gone blind and had died from the domestic product, and others more fortunate had seen their teeth turn black or awakened in the morning to find that they were crippled. Imported liquor, "the real stuff," was in enormous demand. Bootleggers were beginning to swarm the Canadian border by the hundreds. Mexican women were wealthy overnight after crossing the Rio Grande with a carefully suspended cargo of brandy or even tequila inside the very personal zones of their petticoats. Cabin and table stewards aboard the Bermuda-New York passenger lines were reported to be making more each voyage as smugglers than the regular pay of the captains and chief engineers.

No matter how many runs craft like the *Marshall* made, the market for imported liquor would remain. It was an integral part of the new trade. Cut, recut, it still brought the highest prices. Bootleggers were asked incessantly for "good Scotch," "old-time rye," "straight bourbon," "French" brandy and champagne. Without overseas sources, the market might eventually collapse. How long would a man go on drinking home-brew beer or the kind of gin you put together in a bathtub? He had to believe that some of what he sent down his throat was near pre-Prohibition standards.

McCoy was convinced. He agreed to take the *Marshall* into Bimini, the small Bahamian cay close off the Florida coast, and load there for a run to Atlantic City. He would be met by Hain at Bimini. The Vance brothers, another pair of far-sighted speculators like the MacPhersons, had stored a large amount of bonded American bourbon and rye in the cellar of the Bimini Rod and Gun Club, and Hain and his father were their agents.

The load at Bimini for the *Marshall* was fifteen hundred cases of Old Grand Dad. It had been kept under guard in the concrete clubhouse and was stowed fast and neatly aboard. McCoy sailed north on what he knew might be a difficult run. He had no idea of the kind of reception he would get from the police or the Coast Guard in the waters around New York City.

But he brought the schooner up the coast and went to anchor ten miles southeast of Far Rockaway. Then he went ashore and at Tebo's Yacht Basin entered into negotiations with a man named Fred. Delivery, he had decided, would be better in New York than on the beach at Atlantic City. He hired two big motorboats to carry his cargo ashore and Fred established the transportation price at seven dollars a case and promised protection.

McCoy returned aboard, moved the *Marshall* within four miles of

Rockaway Beach and waited for Fred and the motorboats. The night was calm. Fred found the schooner easily and the transfer to the motorboats was made without trouble. Then, McCoy accompanying Fred, they started for a Brooklyn pier.

That was in darkness. Lines were secured and the first boat was unloaded. Then, as work was begun on the second, a police patrol craft rounded the head of the pier and came into the slip. McCoy stood nervously, ready for flight or possible arrest. But a policeman called from the pilot house of the patrol craft, "Leave her until tonight, Fred, She's safe."

The boat, with her load intact, was left, and she was safe. When the unloading was finished with the return of darkness and Fred paid, McCoy sailed joyfully south in the *Marshall*. His doubts were gone. This would last, and he'd end up wealthy. McCoy owned the schooner outright and he had thirty thousand dollars as pay for two voyages. He was not quite ready yet to buy the *Arethusa*, but still the dream was a very close to realization. Then another pleasant thought came to him. Back off New York, in the fashion of John Hancock, he had created a historic precedent. The contraband liquor his vessel had carried was the first to be landed from overseas within the limits of the greatest city in the world.

But along Bay Street in Nassau and in the bars and hotels he visited on his return, he found other Americans who, if not aware of history, were at least determined to make rapid wealth out of Prohibition. Most of them were New Yorkers. They had the sharp, nasal speech to be heard in bookie parlors around Broadway, and in Red Hook and Sands Street. They wore their hatbrims low, their collars were high and shiny, their suits in pronounced patterns, the pants tight, their shoes extremely pointed. When, in the heat of the day or an argument at a bar, they opened their coats, shoulder holsters could be seen. Those held .38-caliber revolvers or the heavier, recently more popular type of weapon, Colt or Luger automatic pistols.

Their talk was tough, and they were tough. Blackjacks projected from certain hip pockets. Brass knuckles were occasionally brought into evidence to prove a point under discussion. McCoy did not like these men. He recognized them as gangsters, and they were here to buy liquor for distribution in the States. He had, as he stood and studied them, a feeling of grave doubt about his trade. If the American gangs took over the rum running business, it would be greatly changed, and in all likelihood highly dangerous.

Then, from among the new arrivals, he was approached by members of an Italian-American syndicate whom he thought he could trust. They offered him a deal that met his haulage rate to sail a load of liquor to be put ashore on Long Island. He took it, checked the cargo, sobered up his crew and sent the *Marshall* again to sea.

He was less reluctant to approach the New York coastline after his Brooklyn experience. Assurances had also been given him by the syndicate, and with bearings on Ambrose Light Ship, then Fire Island Light Ship, he came in close to shore in broad daylight. The transfer onto the flat stretch of beach past Fire Island was openly made. There was no interruption, and McCoy rode in with one of launches, went to New York City.

The syndicate had its headquarters in the Pennsylvania Hotel. The members, when McCoy had been paid, told him they liked his work; he was a good man with a schooner. But he should get himself a bigger boat. One that could carry five thousand cases a trip. The syndicate had just bought a huge amount of Hill and Hill Whiskey in bond at a Kentucky distillery and shipped it to Nassau. McCoy was promised fifty thousand dollars a trip for every five-thousand-case cargo he would bring north to the New York market.

McCoy shook hands with the syndicate members. It was a deal. He left the *Marshall* for his mate to sail back to Nassau. Then he went to Gloucester by train in search of his dream schooner, the *Arethusa*. The future might hold danger with the increase of gang and syndicate control in the trade, but at least he would own her.

He learned in Gloucester that the company which had owned the *Arethusa* was out of business, and she lay idle at Rockland, Maine. He went to Rockland and boarded her, and she was just as beautiful as his dream, perhaps a bit more. The price was twenty-one thousand dollars. He took her out of Rockland and put her into an East Gloucester yard, where he spent another eleven thousand dollars for refit.

She got all new rigging and sails. Topmasts were sent up, and a raking bowsprit shipped. The bowsprit would let her set a flying jib, but he gave her a new motor too, and added a potential ten-thousand dollars in cargo space by changes in her bulkhead plan below deck. Then he had her hull painted white instead of black. He rowed around her where she lay in the fitting slip, and to him she was the pride of Gloucester.

He hired Captain Albert Gott, a veteran New England schooner master, and, remembering the gangster infiltration of Nassau, a collection of really rough fishermen as crew. McCoy then established with Gott, the mate and the crew the pay scale he was to keep later in other vessels he owned. Gott received $1,000 a month for any voyage he made in single command, and $500 a month if McCoy were aboard, with the privilege of carrying $500 worth of liquor at wholesale Nassau prices for his own account. The mate was paid $500 a month when McCoy was not aboard, half that amount when McCoy made the voyage, and had the privilege of stowing $250 in liquor "under the stern" for his own account. The cook, always an important man in any crew, was not forgotten and drew $150 a month in wages and could carry liquor worth an equal sum on each voyage. The sailors got $100 a month and $100 as a bonus at the end of each voyage.

With a full suit of new canvas bent on, the *Arethusa* stood out from Gloucester for Nassau and McCoy took the wheel. He tried her on the wind and off, running on a broad reach or pointed close to the wind, with her big jumbo jib set and without it, and she sailed fine. There was only one thing he regretted about her. When he brought her into Nassau and examined the British ship-registry list he found that another Arethusa was on it. He wanted her under the British flag for protective reasons if caught with a contraband load in American territorial waters, so he renamed her the *Tomoka*. But to him she remained the *Arethusa* and he always called her by that name.

Nassau was thriving with the liquor trade, and ships were scarce that could make the run to the coastal region between Atlantic City and New York, which had begun to be called Rum Row because of the illegal traffic there. McCoy took a fifteen-thousand dollar charter offer for the *Marshall*, saw her loaded and squared away to sea under the command of a man he thought competent to be her captain. This was her first run without him aboard and, unaware of the danger of self-incrimination, he gave the captain detailed written instructions.

He was in a mood of soaring confidence. It did not seem possible that he could miss continued success. His habit was to sit in the coolness of his second-story room in Nassau soon after dawn and watch the *Arethusa* while she took her load aboard. Then he took his bath and let the trade wind dry him slowly as he considered complex plans.

They had grandiose aspects. He saw himself as the owner of a fleet of rum-runners, an operator on an international scale, a man of wealth, who, through shrewd but consistently honest dealing, might get control of the overseas transportation of the trade.

He had nothing except a vague kind of contempt for the gangsters who had begun to infest Nassau. Those men were not even sailors. And neither were they smart in the true sense. Most of their time was spent drinking, gambling and whoring when they were not engaged in plots within plots to steal from each other. They did better with the dice than ship charters, used boasts and threats of violence instead of brains.

McCoy wanted to get back to sea, and aboard the *Arethusa*. But he had the *Marshall* to consider. She would arrive off the New Jersey coast at about the same time he proposed to send the *Arethusa* on a run. If he wanted to make sure of his investments, he should go north by train, meet both vessels. Captain Gott could take the *Arethusa* and her load to sea without him.

McCoy left for Miami, where he was to board a train to New York, right after Captain Gott put the *Arethusa* underway. Gott had no trouble at sea, and with the help of the syndicate whose liquor the ship carried, McCoy was in touch with her when she made her landfall on Montauk Point. But the happy, easy days of Coast Guard interference were past; there was plenty of tacking and night running between the big, tawny headland and Block Island before the patrol craft were eluded and the cargo was out of her and ashore. McCoy was too busy to give much thought to the *Marshall*.

He and the man who acted for the syndicate went ashore happily enough from the *Arethusa* at Block Island. But their business took them to the local telegraph office. Late-news bulletins were stuck with thumbtacks on a wall. McCoy stood and read that the schooner *Henry L. Marshall* had just been seized, with fifteen hundred cases of whiskey aboard, off Atlantic City. William McCoy was named as the owner, and the bulletin stated that the government was searching for another rum runner owned by McCoy and reported as having been seen off Montauk Point.

McCoy said very little to the syndicate agent, but they left the telegraph office at a considerable speed. Then, in a guarded telephone call to New York and the syndicate, McCoy got full possession of the facts. The crew had broached cargo aboard the *Marshall* while at sea, persisted in their sampling after she was off Atlantic City. Then the captain and the mate decided that they should go ashore.

Loud and staggering drunk, they roamed the boardwalk for hours. The young supercargo was the only man aboard still sober, and he was no sailor. When the Coast Guard cutter *Seneca* sighted the schooner, she was slatting back and forth vagrantly with her sails spread. The *Seneca* did not have to challenge twice; she just put a towline aboard and hauled her into New York.

McCoy realized very clearly that he was in immediate danger of arrest. He could, with the written evidence aboard the *Marshall*, be indicted for conspiracy to defraud the Federal government of revenue. His companion had broken into explosive Italian-American language that made sense; they should get to hell out of sight.

He and the syndicate agent set out on foot, found and took refuge with a friendly family. Then, after a call from a pair of unidentified strangers who very likely were revenue agents, they left their hosts. McCoy slipped aboard the Providence steamer, and eventually reached Boston. But he did not feel safe there, and he had information form New York that the *Arethusa* was off Cape Ann. He went to the cape and, at night, out aboard. Captain Gott and the crew gave him a warm welcome, but he had no liking at the moment for American waters. He told Gott to lay a course for Halifax.

Nova Scotia was under a strict Dry law of her own, however, and McCoy decided to move out of Halifax as soon as possible. He spent some time ashore in talk with the French Consul. The small offshore French islands of St. Pierre and Miquelon were given a high recommendation by their representative. No such foolish laws were in effect under the French flag, the consul said. McCoy should take his schooner to St. Pierre, enjoy the island scenery, perhaps make friends with the local merchants who might supply a cargo.

McCoy sailed the *Arethusa* for St. Pierre, but only after he had worked hard to convince Captain Gott and the crew. This was gale season, and cold, bitterly long nor'easters were blowing. The *Arethusa* slogged into them with the helmsman in oilskins and double-lashed at the wheel.

McCoy sat disconsolate in the cabin. He stared at the ruddy sides of the stove while the schooner strained and pitched to the weight of the seas, her canvas chattering. But the helmsman was singing; he sang in broad accents, "Go Feather Your Nest." Then a huge wave came aboard.

The schooner was doused from bow to taffrail. She shook herself and the scuppers sent the wave back into the sea. McCoy looked up through the small opening of the companionway hatch. The helmsman stood soaked, and yet he continued to sing. McCoy laughed with the rhythm of the song. His luck was out for now, no doubt about that. But he was where he belonged, aboard the vessel he loved and at sea.

CHAPTER THREE

St. Pierre was a hospitable place; the people, most of them fishermen, admired the *Arethusa*; and several merchants were willing to make deals for liquor at wholesale prices. McCoy formed contacts and friendships that were to be valuable to him in the future, but he still considered Nassau his base. He waited for a break in the weather and then set the *Arethusa* on her Bahamian course.

Nassau had attracted a great many more American gangsters during his absence, he found. The *Mystery J.*, the old steamer that ran between Nassau and Miami, brought further recruits to the rum running business each time she tied up at the Bay Street quay. These were characters straight from Damon Runyon, but without the charm. They went loud-mouthed, irredeemably profane, from bar to bar. This was only the fall of 1921, but they already called Bay Street "Booze Avenue" and delighted in taunting local constables.

The constables were island Negroes who were sturdy enough and able to take care of themselves in a fight, trained to maintain the law with British quietness and a minimum display of authority. But, in usual colonial style, their uniforms were quite smart: white sun helmets, trim white cotton tunics, cotton gloves and dark blue trousers. The helmets offered an easy target for gin-inspired gangsters, particularly as evening closing time in the bars approached.

There were insults, swiftly passed blows, then the show of blackjacks or automatic pistols. The attitude taken at Government House, however, was that no matter how unruly the new visitors might be, their presence meant vast increase in the island's wealth. Orders were issued to the constabulary to stay out of any fracas, refrain from action except for self-protection or if a British citizen were involved. Then the constables could and should move with all possible force.

"Big Eddie," "Big Harry," "Big Red," "Squinty" and "Lefty" and the rest of the gangsters, as bellicosity began to rise with the ingestion of gin, took to fighting each other. It was simpler that way; more real grudges were settled and no fines had to be paid. The gangsters had chosen, inexplicably, to take over the Lucerne Hotel; it served them as their private battle area and McCoy saw them there at play, at fisticuffs and worse.

He spent time with them for business reasons. He was conspicuous at the bar because of his sun-faded khakis and his preferences for lime squash over gin or rye. But his reputation was known, he was respected and his opinion was asked on many matters relating to liquor prices, charter possibilities and seamanship.

The gangsters, although dispatched to Nassau to transact overseas trade, were wholly ignorant about the sea; not one of them was a sailor. They stood in a kind of abashed awe of McCoy. He in turn was curious to learn how they would solve their shipping problems, and almost equally curious as to why they had chosen the Lucerne as headquarters.

It had been, before their descent, a rather prim establishment. A loosely designed wooden structure with wide porches and galleries, it lay behind a row of palm trees, inside a garden stretching back from Bay Street. Next door was a church. One of the patrons longest in residence was the Chief Justice of the Bahamas, and a number of rooms were taken by families. The owner was a small, gray-haired, bespectacled woman, born and brought up in New England, and named, incredibly, Mrs. Sweeting. She, with her daughter, Gertrude, managed the place. But it was only Mrs. Sweeting who could manage the gangsters. They unfailingly called her "Mother."

Their nightly habit was a dice game in the hotel bar. This sometimes reached the peak of a thousand dollars a point and emotions were aroused. Then there was the cursing, the scuffling, the cries of, "I'll hair-comb ya, ya bastid!" Blackjacks were flourished; brass knuckles left their imprint, and pistol butts creased skulls.

Tommy, the Cockney barman, had a philosophical attitude

regarding such expressions of bad temper, and he ducked down behind the already grievously scarred mahogany and rested his feet. But "Mother" was less disposed to allow damage done to her customers and her establishment. She came in as the conflicts approached climax, walked to the middle of the room and slapped her hands smartly together. She said then, quite calmly, "Boys, boys. If this keeps up, I must ask Tommy to close the bar for the night."

The answer was invariably, "Yeah, Mother."

Then she left. Tommy rose from the rear of the bar and asked who would like what. Blood was stanched. Weapons were put away, and tailoring studied for repair. Drinks were passed, the dice were rattled, bills were tossed and bets covered, but in muted, ashamed voices.

Still, whatever influence "Mother" could exert did not restrain the hoodlums from their most riotous form of relaxation. This was called a "fire dance," and it was supported by general gangster sub-scription. A huge fire was built at early evening in a clearing in the bush past Grant's Town. A drum was made from an empty keg with a cowhide stretched tightly across the top. Cases of gin were stacked and opened for the easy self-service of the dancers. Mulatto girls renowned in Grant's Town as variously accomplished were invited as guests. The drum began to patter, vibrate, roar, and with the fusion of fire and gin, clothing was discarded. When couples tired of dancing, they retired into the darkness and the bush.

The pursuit of such pleasure gained intense popularity. There was a barbaric quality about it which reached deep into the gang-ster psyche. The hoodlums had become real fire-dance fervents, and one night during the absence of "Mother" from the Lucerne, having been borne well past decorum on clouds of gin vapor, they decid-ed to disport themselves in the hotel garden.

Upon Mrs. Sweeting's return near midnight, the fire was touch-ing the palm fronds crimson. The drummer sweated as he banged. Gangsters and girls were far gone in ecstasy, almost naked. She looked up and saw that the rest of her clientele had shuttered their windows against the bacchanalia. It had also been reported to her in Bay Street that in the church alongside the hotel, prayers were being given for the salvation of sinners.

She walked forward through a litter of bottles and clothing.

Then, as the drummer paused, she slapped her hands together in the recognized signal. The hoodlums gaped at her; the girls broke from them and scuttered for their dresses. "You," she told the hoodlums, "go to bed at once." Next she faced the girls. "Run along home. Shoo!" Her glance went to the drummer. "Put out the fire. Pick up those bottles. And take that drum away from here."

Within ten minutes, the Lucerne was so quiet that tree toads could be heard. Shutters were slowly opened. Upstairs, sodden, repentant gangsters snored.

But, though McCoy was amused by Mrs. Sweeting's ability to control the unruly, he had a keen dislike for the financial tactics that some of the gangsters employed against the local merchants. Credit was easily obtainable; Market and Bay Street businessmen saw nothing except sheer profit in the American attempt at Prohibition. They felt safe to take practically any promise of future full payment if five dollars a case were put down as the cost of underwriting the venture.

McCoy was busy with is own concerns. He had recovered a great part of his optimism, regarded his recent experiences along the American coast as no more than bad luck. He had organized what he called the British Transportation and Trading Company, had proposed to buy more schooners cheaply in Nova Scotia for use as rum runners, and had sent Captain Gott in command of *Arethusa* on the way north with a load of rye. Yet he knew that none of his acquaintances at the Lucerne should be entrusted with a cargo that would bring fifty dollars and more per case on Rum Row. The difference between the five-dollar-a-case deposit and the offshore sales price represented too much temptation for men who admittedly had always made their living outside the law. Such credit expansion and inevitable betrayal of those who tendered it would severely injure the trade, McCoy believed. Then his belief was confirmed.

A local merchant named Christie, who had entrusted a gangster combine with seventeen thousand cases for sale on Rum Row, learned that the cargo had been purchased there, but that the combine members would never return and pay him his due share of the profits. Now he was sorely caught, and must pay out of his own pocket the complete initial sale of the cargo. He became sick and soon died; afterwards, any American seeking cargo on credit was met with hard stares.

Then another investor whose liquor had been taken to sea by men who had given only promises to pay for it determined to chase the boat. He hired a seaplane and the pilot flew low over the Florida-bound craft. The liquor owner shouted, shook his fists in gestures of menace, and at last, desperate, fired a revolver. The reply was a burst of rifle shots that made the pilot wonder about the longevity of the flight. He turned back to Nassau and the thieves sailed on for Florida with their cargo.

Some of the bitterness was dissipated, however, when a pair of characters named Squinty and Big Eddie convinced themselves that they were competent to take a vessel to sea. They had bought, after haggling, an ancient and barely navigable sharpie. She looked good to them; they were pleased that they had forced the owner down to their price; and they loaded her to the coamings with rye, set the sails and started for Rum Row, boisterously waving at the Bay Street spectators.

It was a bright afternoon. The water was azure under the sun; the white walls of Fort Montague glistened. Sea birds circled the boat on radiant wings. Squinty and Big Eddie lolled back in the cockpit, content, even a bit drowsy.

The flat-bottomed old sharpie lifted to the first of the trade wind swells at the harbor mouth. She squatted across it. Then the worm-riddled hull creaked, and Squinty and Big Eddie looked down in alarm.

Seams were opening with a gentle, petal-like effect. The bottom was leaving the boat. Plank by plank, it fell away, and where it had been was a surging roil of sea water. The gangsters leaped for the skiff, got in, while, with a soft gurgle, the sharpie submerged. They paddled about, aghast, staring at their cargo. Air bubbles from the cases marked their passage; small fish swam among them in gay processions. The cases settled upon coral close to the cracked, gaping carcass of the sharpie. Shark set gray shadow over them; barracuda darted around the shark. Squinty and Big Eddie knew that the liquor would lie there forever. They locked the oars aboard the skiff and added to their sea experience with the row across the harbor to the Bay Street quay.

But disaster came to McCoy as well as to the pair of amateur navigators. He received word by cable from New York that Captain Gott had suffered a heart attack and died aboard the *Arethusa* while discharging cargo on Rum Row. The captain's death was a great loss to him, and he had no particular confidence in the ability or the sagacity of the mate now in command of the vessel.

He was considering a replacement for Gott when the man he had selected to act as his agent in Nova Scotia returned to Nassau, both penniless and crestfallen. McCoy had entrusted him with a thousand dollars cash as expense money, relied upon him to make the deals for the schooners that would form the new British Transportation and Trading Company fleet. But the agent had gone no further than the dock in Miami before his wallet was stolen. He insisted that, although he was entirely sober at the time, it had been taken from his pocket in broad daylight. Using McCoy's name as credit to buy a ticket, he had left Miami on the next trip of the *Mystery J.* for Nassau, and was not reluctant to admit that he lacked some of the qualities needed to transact business with hard-headed Nova Scotians.

McCoy sat in his room at Mrs. Kemp's and ruefully contemplated this further collapse of his plans. The British Transportation and Trading Company was nothing but figures, names jotted down on slips of paper. It would be well for him to take personal command of *Arethusa* before she, too, was tangled in misfortune. She was one vessel left to him, and to be greatly cherished.

With the *Arethusa* back south, and loading in a cargo of rye, McCoy's hopes were restored. Nassau had become a halcyon town. What the hoodlums called the booze boom had influenced the thinking of even the most tradition-bound Bahamian businessmen. They cited to each other at tea or over a sundowner rum swizzle the figures published by *The Nassau Guardian*.

The government had reported that in the year 1921 the amount of whiskey imported into the colony was estimated at £645,190; gin at £32,633; and ale, beer and porter at £8,299, all told a handsome sum. But in 1922 the whiskey importation was estimated at £932,865; the gin at £43,670; and £14,700 for the milder forms of tipple. These sums were enormously higher than in pre-Prohibition years, and Nassau could look forward along a gleaming vista of prosperity to many civic improvements, among them a new water system.

Merchants broke the somnolent habits that had existed since the end of the blockade-runner era of the American Civil War. A number of them enlisted as representatives for British distillers. Quite a few, but with more discretion than was shown by the pioneer speculators, entered the trade themselves; they supplied cargoes for the vessels making the runs to Rum Row. Others drew upon their own sea knowledge, bought boats, manned them with crews recruited from the island sponge fishers, put cargoes aboard and supercargoes to keep the tally and handle the cash, and sent the liquor north for direct Rum Row sale.

Even a member of the ministry felt the call to fortune. The reverend Mr. Dunn, who had worked long years at the propagation of the gospel through the Out Islands, resigned to become the master of a rum-runner. He cruised far in search of cargo at reasonable prices, put in at St. Pierre and Miquelon, touched Halifax when Nova Scotia revoked its Dry Law, was frequently on Rum Row and, canny in his dealings with the shoreside people, became very successful.

The Anglican bishop, the example of ex-Reverend Dunn before him, was persuaded to sell the stout, bluff-bowed schooner that for decades had carried loads of Bible tracts to the islanders. She still kept her churchly name, *Messenger of Peace*, when she went into the rum running business. Her new owner was a Cockney name Loumans who sailed her with his wife as mate and two former fishermen as deckhands.

Captain Loumans installed a forty-five horsepower motor in the *Messenger of Peace*, stowed a rye-whiskey load and made good his course for Ocracoke Inlet, below Cape Hatteras. This was the tricky shoal-water region where the blustering pirate Teach, better known as Blackbeard, had gone aground and, rather than surrender, had been killed in a fight with the law. Captain Loumans circumnavigated the shoals with care and, when he grounded at last, was very circumspect. He slid two cases of whisky soundlessly over the stern for the crew of the Coast Guard patrol boat that pulled his craft clear into the channel. The county sheriff, however, was more adamant; he arrested the captain and his wife.

Loumans made an appeal to the sheriff on the basis of compromise and it was accepted. He would sleep in the jail each night, also keep it clean, and he and his wife would provide their own food, if she were permitted to tend the *Messenger of Peace*. The Loumans were eventually awarded two months off for good behavior and, with the best wishes of the sheriff and shouts to return soon from the citizens, they sailed for Nassau to take another load aboard and bring it to Ocracoke.

Their entry into Nassau, and their subsequent quick departure, gave added incentive to the trade. The harbor was now cluttered with rum-runners, and they formed a weird flotilla. There were former yachts which were hastily loading for a trip, and subchasers that had served the United States Navy and still wore their wartime gray paint with daubs over the bow numerals, and tugboats called from backwater retirement. A group of men just in from Cuba told the story that a Spanish cruiser, which had last done duty in the Spanish-American War and since rusted on the beach, had been towed off for minor repairs. Her hull and her boilers had been lightly patched, one of her compasses adjusted, her coal bunkers filled. She, too, was bound for Rum Row.

But the Nassauvian authorities had reached the end of their patience about harbor conditions. They chased all rum-carrying craft out of Nassau Harbor to nearby Salt Cay, let them retain that as an anchorage. The *Arethusa* was there among the motley the day she was attached, claimed by another "owner." The mate and her crew were aboard; McCoy was soon notified in Nassau.

He had been aware for some months that he was under indictment in the United States as a consequence of the seizure of the *Marshall*. A Bahamian lawyer had counseled him that his British registry for the *Arethusa* was not enough. His possession of her would be much safer if he were to make some British subject the titular owner.

McCoy chose for the purpose an Englishman named Johnson, who was living in Nassau. Johnson expressed agreement with the plan and took three thousand dollars as payment. But, after the ownership papers were made out to him, Johnson claimed the *Arethusa* as his own.

McCoy called on the lawyer, who said that he firmly believed that

McCoy should let the schooner go. A legal fight in the Bahamian courts would only involve him in further difficulties. The lawyer gave him to understand that he had a completely objective attitude towards the case. He represented both parties; Johnson was also his client.

McCoy did not take any more of the lawyer's time. He went to Mrs. Kemp's for a Colt pistol he had brought for protective reasons when on Rum Row. The Colt inside his trousers waistband, he sought Johnson. He brought the muzzle close against Johnson's abdomen after he found him. Their talk was brief, but he was able to convince the other man that he, McCoy, was the owner of the *Arethusa*. They parted then and McCoy felt a sudden, compulsive desire to get aboard the schooner and be at sea.

Among the liquor dealers flourishing in Nassau was an American named George Murphy. He was a bulky man, no more than five feet, seven inches in height and over three hundred pounds in weight. His statement about himself was that the only things he could buy ready-made for his wardrobe were handkerchiefs. But he had an acute business sense, and sold, in McCoy's opinion, the best rye whiskey available to the Rum Row trade.

McCoy had a stowage capacity of five thousand cases aboard the *Arethusa* and yet, at the time, only enough cash to purchase a thousand-case lot. He went to Murphy for it. The broad-beamed dealer had in his warehouse whiskey that was from seven to ten years old. It had evaporated to an average of twenty-eight gallons within each of the charred oak casks that contained it, and Murphy reduced it to one hundred proof with distilled water. The stuff was then bottled and labeled and sent to the packaging tables. Negro women who sang hymns in sweet voices made up the "hams" for sea stowage. Six bottles, each in its paper wrapping, were stacked in the compact pyramidal form, straw placed around them and a close cover of burlap stitched with double sail twine.

McCoy paid Murphy, saw his load put onto the drays, took a hack to accompany it to the lighterage dock. The donkeys that pulled the drays shambled easily over the cobbles. Their drivers sang or played mouth organs, and the favorite tunes were "God Save the King" and "Verily I Say unto You." The lighter men sang, too, crossing the harbor. They called good luck as McCoy told the mate to get the anchor up and sails bent on for sea.

He had fair weather while he ran north. Eight days after he cleared Nassau, he picked up the powerful beam of Fire Island Light Ship and worked his way in to an anchorage in the midst of the Rum Row congregation. The fleet now maintained position a full twenty miles offshore after a number of Coast Guard arrests and seizures within the three-mile limit. Here the big white cutters kept no more than a nominal guard, their real intent to catch the small craft that came out from shore with the darkness to buy and load.

McCoy lacked a consignee for his cargo. He sold over the side to any buyer who pitched his money, the bills neatly rolled and clasped within a rubber band, onto the deck. Murphy's rye was popular; thousand cases sold fast. There was little delay, and McCoy was glad. A cell in a Federal jail was waiting for him over there on the mainland if he were picked up, he knew. But he was back in Nassau eighteen days after he left, his financial condition distinctly improved.

CHAPTER FOUR

McCoy was given to some reflection during his next stay in Nassau. It was caused by his conversations with the United States consul, Lorin A. Lathrop. The officer was about to end a long career in the consular service. He had worked and lived in many countries, was a man of culture, a writer, also a painter. Under the pseudonym of Kenyon Gambier he had written a considerable amount of fiction; the magnificent color qualities of the Bahamian sea and sky and beaches and the great grace of the people sent him often to his easel, and he had asked for the assignment in anticipation of quiet, easy duty.

But McCoy challenged both his official and private life. His consular work demanded that he do all in his power to stop McCoy, already under Federal indictment, from further violation of the Prohibition law. Then, after the consulate was shut for the day, he and McCoy would meet. The gray-headed, soft-spoken government officer and the strapping, sea-brown schooner owner were good friends, despite vast dissimilarities.

Lathrop was always firm, no matter how the conversation might turn, in his belief that McCoy should give up rum running. He pointed out the losses that McCoy had suffered and the eventual certainty of capture if McCoy persisted in his runs to Rum Row. The chances were too big, Lathrop said. McCoy should get straight with the law, take what profits he had left and go into a honest trade.

McCoy laughed at him. He told Lathrop that he was doing fine. And he still was not convinced that the Prohibition law was just; the majority of the American people were against it and he simply satisfied their desires for a decent drink of whiskey. But, as Lathrop pursued the debate with gentle stubbornness, McCoy was forced to accept some of the consul's statements.

The gangster influence was now almost entirely dominant in the trade. These men not only ran liquor into the States. They had no scruples whatsoever; they carried dope on their trips north, were known to take live cargoes from Cuba and smuggle in Chinamen at two thousand dollars a head. The usual price asked by a smuggler was one thousand dollars cash, paid in advance, the balance after the Chinese were ashore Stateside. McCoy had been approached many times to sail with such cargo; he was well aware of the terms. He was aware, too, that this year, 1922, the former Bahamian sponge schooner *Mary Beatrice* had been found adrift at dawn between Rum Row and New York Harbor.

Her crew were gone. There was no sign of them. Down in the hold, however, very silent and stained with blood that did not come from any wounds they bore, were nine Chinamen. They maintained their silence until deported. It was only the supposition of the Coast Guard and the Immigration Service that the crew had lost courage, tried to destroy the passengers at the last moment before arrest. The Chinamen had been too strong and the crew had been pitched over the rail instead, ridden the tide to sea.

McCoy told Lathrop that his scruples would never let him deal in either narcotics or aliens. But there was a dream schooner bigger and faster than the *Arethusa* which he wanted to have built, and when she was finished he would sail her to the South Seas. That meant a lot of money. He could only make it rum running. So he'd stick with the trade. He and the consul smiled at each other and parted, and the next morning McCoy called on George Murphy to arrange for a new load.

He bought two thousand cases of Murphy's rye and stowed it aboard, started to get the *Arethusa* ready for sea. Then, at the Lucerne, he entered into conversation with some of the gangster patrons. It would be the season of greatest sales on Rum Row, they pointed out to him. He was prevailed upon to take thirty-seven hundred cases of their liquor in addition to his own. It was now the month of December; he would meet winter gales and severe conditions throughout his time on the Row. The total cargo load was far in excess of what the schooner should carry. Still, McCoy decided to put to sea with it; he was willing to gamble the schooner for the profit to be made.

The stuff was brought aboard from lighters. He filled the hold with "hams" until the hatch cover almost jammed as it was tugged shut. He stowed more under the focsle floor, under the cabin floor and beneath the cabin bunks. The loading finished, he went ashore to Mrs. Kemp's for a solid shoreside sleep-in; he would need all his energy at sea. The run to Rum Row was doubtless going to be a serious ordeal.

Mrs. Kemp protested to him, when he left the house the next day, that the schooner was overloaded. He grinned at her in farewell and hired a fisherman to row him out aboard. But here in the sunlit harbor at broad noon the *Arethusa* seemed to ride quite low. When he paid off the fisherman and stepped aboard he stood on a wet deck. The vessel was so deeply loaded that her scupper ports were awash.

McCoy faced his sailing master, an old-time Royal Navy veteran named Crosby, and his crew. They were glum, pensive. McCoy turned the powers of his persuasion upon Crosby; he was able to get the captain to admit that he still thought the schooner seaworthy. But one of the crew said, "We'll be on the Row in January. She'll ice up and sink right under us."

That, McCoy had already considered; it was not at all impossible. But he had the classic question for them: "Any of you boys afraid?"

Nobody answered him. Seamanly pride had been exposed. McCoy spoke fast. "I'll ship three more focsle hands. That'll make it easier up north."

The crew spokesman said, half smiling, "You put three more men aboard her, Captain Bill, she'll sink right here."

But McCoy returned to shore and found three more sailors. They were Finns, big men with malletlike hands and a thirst gained while working in a lumber schooner. Rum Row under winter conditions represented no particular difficulty to them. McCoy took them aboard at once, and made sure they had their seabags with them. Then he told Crosby to haul anchor, set sail before the Finns or any of the other men chose to take lifesaving practice by a swim to the beach.

Arethusa surged over the bar at high tide and Crosby put her due north with a fine, fresh southeasterly breeze. All canvas was spread; she kicked the sapphire sea into creaming white foam with her fore-foot; the taffrail log gave her speed as twelve knots. She sailed supremely well even with the extreme load. But McCoy pondered the effects of the weather past the Hole in the Wall and Abaco Island.

She ran on handsomely, with surprising freedom of motion, through the Northwest New Providence Channel, the helmsman and the watch on deck bare to the waist. Then, with Abaco Light above the horizon, McCoy gave the order to secure for what was to come. Anything that was movable on deck was strongly lashed. Double tarpaulins were stretched on the hatches, tightly battened down, the wedges driven hard.

Now she was at the Hole in the Wall and through, Abaco astern, the wide Atlantic expanse ahead. McCoy made the gesture that had become customary aboard rum-runners bound for the Row in winter-time. He set a wooden rack in front of the helmsman. It contained four bottles from which the man could choose: wine, rum, rye and Scotch.

But the *Arethusa* sailed with fair weather that lasted for days. No real stress was put upon her until she was three hundred miles from Cape Hatteras. A heavy south-westerly storm hit her then, and she was caught laboring by immense waves. Captain Crosby took the wheel while McCoy and the hands fought to bring in the mainsail.

Crosby stared at the waves as they tumbled, gray-maned with spindrift. He balanced the wheel spokes, eased off, came back, eased again, eased once more and three waves had passed in suc-cession. That should mean a lull in which he could send the schooner up to the wind.

It came. He swung the wheel spoke after spoke and she lay pointed exactly into the eye of the storm. Hove to like this, howev-er, she pitched in great, staggering descents. When she righted, she rolled her beams under and the men dragging at the somber pin-nacle of canvas were almost slung over the side. Suction from the wave recoil took their feet out from under them. They clung to the reef points, to the boom or a shroud, to the canvas itself.

Then a monster wave swept over the bow. It was so huge the jumbo jib and foresail were battered by the solid mass. The strong-hulled dories in their lashings were rent; the flotsam pieces spun darkly with the wave crest towards the men. They ducked, heads down, not breathing, numbly hoping, waiting.

The wave left them. They felt the deck beneath the slop of water inside their seaboots and the sail was still to be furled. McCoy shouted against the clamor made by the wind, the sea and the canvas. They heard him and they bunched the sail, passed the canvas stops into place and lashed it fast.

Arethusa still carried foresail and jib. Captain Crosby had the wheel hard down and she would not respond; she drifted as though derelict. McCoy and the men were afraid to go below. They hunkered wordlessly, backs to the weather, along the main boom, trying to squirm their oilskins collars high, their sou'westers low over their necks. All of them were wet through every layer of clothing. The wind pierced and was bitterly cold. They would freeze if they kept on sitting here. McCoy, the nondrinker, made the suggestion: "Let's go below and get a drink."

The men were with him, in absolute, immediate accord. But darkness had come, the deck was treacherously slippery and waves tore at their legs as they stood to run for the companionway hatch. The men ran alone, each in his turn. They grasped the companionway slide, shoved it open, jumped and sprang below before the rush of the next wave, thrust the slide shut and sat panting on the steps.

McCoy broached a bottle of rye. It went rapidly as the men drank. Then they sat there and stared and listened. They were bounced with the gyratory heaving of the schooner. She rose and fell off from the waves, smothered and then freed herself, and bucked at the lashed wheel. The men did not talk much; there was little for them to say. Death was still very close, and they all felt the awful, claustrophobic fear common to deck seamen when penned below.

They watched each other in the flickering of the gimbaled cabin lantern, tried to discern in the wind-reddened faces some sign of hope rather than fear. McCoy and Crosby studied the barometer and repeatedly read the passage of time on the bulkhead clock. A sea sweat was around the rubber gaskets at the porthole deadlights; a small trickle was down the ladder steps from the companionway hatch, but the cabin, seemingly the entire vessel, remained sound and dry.

McCoy counted the seconds between the wave impacts, and

there were more; the waves were breaking further apart. The storm velocity had also lessened. The high intense yowl that tortured the eardrums was now gone from the wind. McCoy asked for men to venture on deck with him.

Several volunteered. They scrambled forward on hands and knees from the companionway. The big jib, a new sail when bent on, was blown completely out of the bolt ropes. The foresail was a black, rigid mass that took the pelting of the sprays with a sound like a hammer upon steel. Across the toss of the wave crests, dawn showed in a lemon-green rind at the horizon.

McCoy and the sailors doused the foresail. They replaced it with a small riding sail and the schooner lay easier to the waves. Then they went back to the cabin to dry out, massage the ache from their hands. Frenchy Rivert, the cook, was at the stove in the galley. He worked with acrobatic skill, braced wide-legged over the frying pan and coffee pot. He gave the men ham and eggs and mugs of coffee that erased the need for sleep.

Watches were set. A sailor went to the wheel. McCoy checked the pump and there was nothing except a very small discharge from the bilge bottoms. She had stayed dry throughout, was in fine shape, and none of the crew had received serious harm. McCoy turned in; his faith in the *Arethusa* had been proven, and now, the worst of the storm well past, he could sleep.

But in the fair weather the next day, Captain Crosby was gravely injured. The sailing master was about to leave the cabin and come on deck when a preventer backstay let go, weakened by the storm. Crosby was climbing the companionway ladder; he did not have a chance as the heavy preventer block dropped vertically from aloft. He was struck upon the back of the skull, knocked sagging into a coma.

McCoy examined him in the cabin. The bone of the skull was frightfully dented; the pulse was very slow. Here was the problem that so often confronted crews aboard vessels which did not carry a doctor. All McCoy had as a guide was what he called "the doctor book," really little more than a pamphlet.

One paragraph contained the instructions for the care of a case of brain concussion. Those were to keep the patient's feet warm and bathe the face with vinegar and water. McCoy and Frenchy Rivert placed Crosby close to the cabin stove. They massaged his feet; they bathed his face; but the state of coma remained deep.

The sea was beginning to rise with the arrival of gale-force wind. McCoy ordered the *Arethusa* hove to under a spare jumbo jib and the reefed foresail. He and Rivert kept steadily on at their treatment of the injured man. But in the travail of the gale, Crosby died. McCoy found himself unable to perform the burial service. Fair weather once more, the sea calm, he gave the duty to Rivert. It was the cook who stood solemnly on deck and, with his broad French-Canadian accent, read from the Bible and committed the body.

An American flag was used. Bars of lead that had been taken from the ballast were at the feet. The men rested in silence, caps at their sides, in two straight rows beside the hatch board from which the body plunged. Then, at McCoy's nod, they went back to work. Full, correct ceremony had been tendered their shipmate.

The *Arethusa* entered fog off Barnegat. It was a dismal beat up along the coast to Rum Row. The course McCoy followed was taken from what Fulton Market fishermen called, "The Gully," the vast and winding gorge the Hudson River had cut into the sea floor. A man at the bow swung the hand lead every fifteen minutes, reported his soundings to McCoy beside the wheel. When the lead gave thirty fathoms, McCoy knew he was over "The Gully" and right on course.

McCoy checked chart, compass and time, and gazed into the bleak gray barriers of the fog across the grim darkness of the sea. He told himself that the cargo aboard was worth $171,000 and was one of the most valuable to be delivered upon the Row. When sold, it would be purchased for double that, and then the price would be doubled again by the bootleggers ashore. It came out at $684,000, a considerable fortune for any man. But in the chill night, the fog wraiths around him as he strained to keep course, he wondered why he had chosen this trade. There would be gales and heavy seas, the imminent danger of collision on the Row. He would be forced to run the *Arethusa* out into the Atlantic and clear of the ship lanes that converged off New York to keep her from being rammed blindly at night. And Crosby was dead, and Crosby had been a good man, a real sailor. While he was in the mood to admit it, his friend, the consul, Lorin Lathrop, had made a great deal of sense.

Bill McCoy: This is in the great Golden Age days as the *Arethusa* loads at Nassau.

For the Go-through guys: McCoy with machine gun on the afterdeck of the *Arethusa* at sea.

Fair Weather: Guests at dinner aboard the *Arethusa* while bound north for the Row. The woman is the famous Gertrude Lythgoe, known in Nassau, and rightly, as "Queen of the Bootleggers."

The *Arethusa*: Sweetest of the schooner lot to run to the Row.

Whisper No More: The *Whispering Winds* at New London after capture. After conversion she became Coast Guard patrol boat *CG-986*. (*U.S. Coast Guard Photo*)

Mary, a typical contact boat, at Greenport, Long Island, New York. This 43-footer was powered with a 100-horsepower engine. (*U.S. Coast Guard Photo*)

Unloading contraband from a captured rum-runner. *(U.S. Coast Guard Photo)*

The deck of the rum-runner *Kirk and Sweeney*. Following her capture she was converted into the U.S. Coast Guard Academy training vessel *Chase*. *(U.S. Coast Guard Photo)*

Rum-runner *Mary Langdon* in New Bedford, Massachusetts, flanked by the cutters *Redwing*, left, and *CG-237*, right; guarding after her seizure. *(U.S. Coast Guard Photo)*

Coast Guard destroyer *Beale* trails an unidentified rum schooner. *(U.S. Coast Guard Photo)*

CHAPTER FIVE

The stubborn, almost desperate determination to get rid of their cargoes at a profit kept the Rum Row vessels in their ragged line during that winter of 1922-23. Gales swooped from the northeast, then the northwest, and blew for weeks at a time. Ice clogged the decks, hung in heavy frescoes from the rigging, sheathed cabins and bulwarks and hull sides. The strange flotilla rode perilously though the huge seas.

Many of the rum-runners were lost. The usual practice was to anchor while waiting for the contact boats from shore. But nearly all the craft were ill-found, their gear in bad shape or insufficient. Anchor cables parted and ships veered down in the snow-pelted darkness upon their neighbors. Men yelled, tried to fend off, and wood smashed and steel buckled; crews were in the freezing water without a chance of being saved.

The greater danger, however, was that of collision with the hundreds of ships which regularly plied in and out of the port of New York. This was the areas called by sailors "Broadway and Forty-second Street" because of the density of the traffic. The Rum Row craft lay squarely at the convergence of transatlantic and coastwise courses. Each night meant extreme hazard. The rum-runners carried no anchor lights, rang no bells, failed to sound foghorns in order to escape detection by the Coast Guard. They were all but invisible under the ice that blurred their low silhouettes.

Passenger ship masters seeking anxiously for Ambrose Light Ship heard the sudden, exclamatory triple clang of the lookout's bell on the fo'c'sle-head. There was a brief image across the lenses of the night glasses trained from the bridge: a stub mast, dark, staggering figures that waved wildly as they ran the icy deck far below, grasped life rings or tried to heave a dory out of the chocks on the cabin topside. Then there was the crunch of impact, the quick grind and shiver of disintegration under the onrush of the forefoot. Sometimes a random cry rose, as vague as the mewing of a gull.

Tankers bound in from the Gulf with full winter loads struck down their toll. Colliers, slower but still no more capable of helping survivors, rammed and sank barely seen craft and were forced to keep on course to avoid further collision. Even the Coast Guard cutters assigned to Rum Row patrol steered swiftly changing courses to save themselves, the officer of the watch tensely staring ahead for another boat that he might miss. With dawn, as the tide came in, beachcombers between Sandy Hook and Sea Bright had good pickings. Often a loose bottle, an unsmashed case of Scotch or rye could be lifted from the undertow. Money was found in sodden pockets, too, for those who failed to find liquor and didn't mind groping among the bodies of the drowned.

McCoy made it his habit aboard *Arethusa* to run far out to sea each night. He took her as much as a hundred miles offshore and after daylight, the northers still blowing, made good speed back. But while on the Row during the hours of light he still refused to anchor. The schooner kept an easier motion under sail; he jogged her at two or three knots along the coast, waiting for a break in the weather and the arrival of the contact boats.

When the weather subsided a bit, McCoy's brother Ben came out in a launch that sent spray clouting high; she wallowed with a load that was very welcome to the schooner crew. Aboard the *Arethusa*, they were drawing on their last tank of fresh water. Ben brought that, and also crates of fresh vegetables, a quarter of beef, cigarettes, newspapers and magazines. There was no radio in the schooner, and the men, sick of each other and each other's life histories and attempts at humor, were almost as eager for the reading matter as the provisions. Frenchy Rivert went quickly to the galley stove with a great chunk of the beef and the vegetables. While the meal cooked, the men took time out to hang the rest of the quarter of beef in the rigging. Several more meals would be served from it, they knew, and they had lived long enough on what Frenchy could do with the contents of cans.

Ben McCoy had good news for his brother. The bootleg-liquor market was thriving. The contact boats waited only for a diminution of storm conditions to make the run to the Row and load. But ice was thick in the inlets alongshore. Most of the contact boats, for reasons of speed, were lightly constructed. Tidal flow brought chunks of ice forth from the inlets, and recently a fast sixty-footer had ripped her hull planking through as she sailed the North River off Hoboken. She had five hundred cases of rye aboard and a crew of three men, and was being exerted to her maximum speed. Ice gashed the planking like a vast sidelong axe blow. She sank at once, crew, liquor, boat sucked deep into the somber river. Commuters, Ben said, were still pointing out the spot as they went on their daily round to Manhattan aboard the Jersey Central ferries. The price of smuggled liquor should go up, and plenty, for the chances a man had to take in running it to shore.

Bill McCoy fully agreed. When the contact boats came out, their crews engaged in enormous risk. They gambled upon the weather, evasion of the Coast Guard, the seaworthiness of the boats, the stability of motor performance, the escape from arrest alongshore upon return. But they were for the most part excellent seamen, born on this stretch of coast, accustomed to its gales and fogs and cruel undertows, confident they could overcome them. Before Prohibition, they had been fishermen, worked as seiners or cod liners, served in the oyster boats, hauled lobster pots, tonged the clam beds in the bluefly-wretched waters of Barnegat Bay. Here was a better living than they had ever made or would very probably ever make again, and each load run in successfully brought double the initial investment.

Their favorite craft were the famous Jersey sea skiffs. These were built on the dory principle but with a flat, transom stern and shallow draft. The usual length was twenty-eight feet overall, the beam fairly broad, the engine commonly a sixty-horsepower, six-cylinder Pierce Arrow taken from an automobile and installed in a watertight compartment. Wide open, the boats light, the engines could turn up fifteen knots; loaded, they made about half that. A Coast Guard picket boat could catch them when they carried a load, but the motor exhausts were under water, gave little if any sound at low speed.

Two men formed the core of each crew. One man handled the

helm and the motor control while his partner worked the big gal-vanized-tin fisherman's pump that sent the spray that leaped aboard gushing back into the sea. The boats ranged forth in anything like reasonably fair weather from the Navesink River and Raritan Bay, Keyport Harbor, Cheesequake Creek and Arthur Kill while daylight lasted. Some kept together in threes and fours, to veer off on sepa-rate courses in case of Coast Guard pursuit and thus avoid capture; others ran by themselves, straight for the Row. The fast-riding boats splattered the gray winter seas with foam. The motors gave a thrum-ming roar through the wind, and the forehulls, high with the speed thrust, sent a slap-slap-slap like clapping of thousands of hands.

The Row got ready for trade. Wooden signs, hand-lettered by the crews, were hung in the rigging; they gave the prices of the various kinds of liquor for sale. The contact boats drew close with the fall of darkness, their men watching for Coast Guard craft but also the prices. Then lines were tossed, fenders were put over, the names of brands and amounts shouted, and the loading started.

Money was pitched aboard the *Arethusa* in the usual style, a roll of big-denomination bills held together by an elastic band. McCoy was forced to count fast; many of the bills were thousand-dollar, and some five-thousand-dollar; he could do no more than squint hurriedly at them, slide them into the drawer of the desk in the cabin or between the pages of his *American Practical Navigator*, and hope they were not counterfeit. But he was given bad bills only once.

Those were in a roll of twenties offered by a man who was in a great hurry to be gone. McCoy, who believed in the maintenance of public relations, had the habit at the end of each transaction of mak-ing a gift of a free case. The man with the twenty-dollar bills did not wait for his, however, but cast off and started wide throttle for shore. McCoy took another look at the money under the cabin lantern; the stuff, even to his untrained eye, was suspicious.

Arethusa held slight headway, had been jogging back and forth as the deal was made. McCoy ordered more canvas hoisted and set a course in pursuit. He talked with a pair of gangsters whom his Lucerne Hotel acquaintances had insisted on putting aboard on the Row to protect their share of the cargo. Ben McCoy had brought them out from New York on one of his supply trips and until now they had been a woeful, useless duo. Their seafaring prior to boarding the schooner had been between the Battery and Coney Island. During the long offshore runs the *Arethusa* made at night they lay, too weak to be profane, in their bunks in the fo'c'sle, retched each time the crew spoke of food. But when told of counterfeit money given in exchange for good liquor owned in part by the gang they represented, they prepared themselves. They went on deck with their hats jammed low, pistols in the side pockets of their tight double-breasted overcoats. They'd show the sonofabitch how to be honest.

McCoy and his crew were also armed. Back in Nassau, as a simple precaution against what might happen on the Row, he had issued each man a Colt pistol, and he kept one within his own reach. The passer of the false twenties was overhauled long before he was able to get to shore. The gangster pair in their strongest, non-seasick voices advised him of his error. They indicated vividly what their enfilade could do to him, and then suggested restitution in legal currency. McCoy added a few words of advice, and without much protest, the exact sum was paid, each bill studied to be sure it was authentic. Then, no hopes for a future meeting expressed, McCoy took the *Arethusa* back to her station on the Row.

Foul weather persisted, and McCoy felt sea fatigue; he was again relatively wealthy and content to hold eight hundred cases that belonged to him for a later sale. He left the *Arethusa* towards the end of January and gave her over to a sailing master with orders to meet him in Canada. Then he slipped ashore undetected, went on to New York and, after a quiet train trip, banked $127,000 in Halifax. He was still attracted by the trade, would continue in it. Why not, with the money he had just deposited? He returned to Nassau aboard the schooner and formed plans to make another run.

The summer of 1923 was to become an idyl in his memory. Spring had been fine, with a regular performance of schedule: a week to load in Nassau, a week under weigh to the Row, a week to sell, then a week back to the Bahamas to reload. But summer was matchless. It was, although McCoy in no wise sensed the fact, the peak season for Rum Row, would never be equaled by him or any other smuggler.

The weather was magnificent, with long periods of calm, only enough cloud to obscure the moon and enough night mist to confuse the Coast Guard as the laden contact boats shoved off for shore. The *Arethusa* had her own generator and McCoy burned a brilliant light at the masthead truck, put a barrel beneath it to cast the radiance upward, outward, advertise the position of the vessel and still leave her decks in shadow.

From the onset of dusk over the Jersey hills and the towers of Manhattan until, at three o'clock, the boardwalk at Asbury Park was darkened, was the time of greatest activity. The contact boats surged forth from shore by the hundreds. They cut broad wake patterns past Old Orchard and Romer Shoals, whipped clear from the beams of Sandy Hook Light, were discreet about their use of the illumination rendered mariners by Scotland Light Ship, took the same care with Ambrose Light Ship, plunged into the open sea swell, and still at full throttle, came abreast of the Rum Row fleet.

The *Arethusa* had as many as fifteen customers at a time. No engine was shut down; the boat skippers were ready for instant flight. The boats clunked hull to hull around the schooner, pitching, yawing, settling to their loads. The motor concatenation made a shout hard to hear on deck, and the men were under extreme tension as they swung the burlocks from the hatch to the rails, across the rails to the cockpits being stowed. But McCoy's mate was at the mainmast crosstrees with a pair of night glasses; he kept the deck informed of any Coast Guard movement.

Men known to McCoy made their own cargo transferal. They put the money into his hands or tossed the rolls of bills and told him the amounts, the brands taken. "Here's three grand for five hundred Johnnie Walker Black... I got four hundred of Dewar's Bill, and I'll top off with a hundred of Booth's High and Dry. Pay you the next time I'm on deck... Got Golden Wedding and the count is right and this squares for it. So long, Bill."

McCoy stood, his shirt stuck to his back with sweat, in the gentle night breeze. When his hands and his pockets and the slack in the front of his shirt were full he went below to the cabin and got rid of the money. He didn't bother to count closely; he had to trust these men. The bills pushed between the pages of the *Navigator* or into the desk drawer, he hurried back up the ladder on deck.

Some men, when he questioned them, admitted they were

hungry. Frenchy Rivert fed them beside the foremast while they stared at the sea, watching for the Coast Guard. Others took a fast drink from the bottle McCoy offered. All accepted the free case, nodded, smiled, said their thanks before they cast off the lines and worked the boats without stridence away into the darkness.

McCoy and his crew, nearly every crew on the Row, were exhausted by dawn. During the space of one frantic night, between the hours of five and ten, McCoy sold thirty-four hundred cases of liquor, saw them taken over the side and started for shore. When he dropped into his bunk, he had no clear idea of the sum of money aboard. It stuffed the desk drawer, protruded like the leaves of a bizarre cabbage plant from the *Navigator* and lumped his pockets. He must take the risk of carrying it ashore in a suitcase, he knew, in the same way he had other recent payoffs. The cabin lantern still burning, he slept.

But daytime held delight for the Rum Row fleet. The vessels had ventured in so close that with good visibility the slender white reach of the Woolworth Tower could be seen. Arrangements had been made by satisfied customers ashore for the delivery of fresh milk and newspapers each morning. The fleet disported itself after a minimum of necessary work was done. Visitors were frequent.

Mackerel boats fished close alongside. They stopped on their way in to Fulton Market and a portion of the new catch was swapped for a case or two. When the Coast Guard patrol craft were at the other end of the Row, scallopers took as much as twenty-five cases aboard, part cash and part catch in payment. Lobstermen bartered the short-tails which would have no particular value ashore but to a smuggler were worth a quart apiece. The fleet enjoyed a sea-food cuisine that, the cooks said, "couldn't be bought for five dollars a plate in the big fancy Broadway joints, I betcha."

Then news of men with lots of money but no women to spend it for them brought a different kind of visitor. Among them were amateurs, but they were outnumbered by professionals who came from as far away as Atlantic City and Yonkers and were escorted by companions with silk shirts, snap-on bow ties and hard eyes. Impromptu galas were staged on deck. The latest, one-piece Annette Kellerman bathing suits were exhibited while sailors incited by lust and whiskey climbed the crosstrees and dived overside in their drawers.

Gramophones of the crank-handle type, supplied by the more music-minded pimps, played fox trots, waltzes, polkas. There was cheek-to-cheek dancing on the afterdeck; an amateur from Perth Amboy lost her status when she stroked her ukulele and then sang, "How You Gonna Keep 'Em Down on the Farm?" Mixed bathing ended in intimate interviews in the fo'c'sles, then paid-for fornication, no whiskey discount allowed.

The revelry was interrupted by the arrival of "Music," the hopeful pilot of an accident-wracked seaplane. Music was on the Row not for pleasure but for financial advancement, and he hoped he could get his machine back into the air again with its load before the Coast Guard seized him. Twenty-five cases, his maximum load capacity, were rowed out to him in a dory and he stowed them and paid and tried batting the old pusher propeller. The big Coast Guard cutter *Seminole* had spotted him and Music's time to take off was very short. He batted again, and the motor refused again, but finally it sputtered and gave power. He made his run over the calm water and put the biplane awkwardly into the air, saluted the cheering whores and smugglers and headed into the sunset.

The whores, their own mission accomplished on a local basis, rejoined the regatta conducted by the pimps to the vessels further along the Row. Word of their presence had spread before them. Crews stood shaven, bathed, cleanly dressed and money in hand at the rails. No business except personal business would be done tonight. With the inflaming of fresh passion and renewal of the bottles, national songs were sung before the fo'c'sles were occupied. Strains of "Allouette, Gentille Allouette!" rose from the crews that hailed from St. Pierre and Miquelon. Veterans of the Royal Canadian Navy let go with "I've Got Sixpence, Jolly, Jolly Sixpence," and their compatriots from the Bahamas told the night that all Mama wanted was shandy, shandy, brandy all the time. Swedes, Danes and Finns had mouth organs or accordions, and it pleased them to do polkas and a little singing, a less amount of dancing until they and their guests repaired below. Yankees out of the New England ports were at a loss; public carnal amusement was against their grain, but they could sing, "Brighten the Corner Where You Are," and that one about "How You Gonna Keep 'Em Down on the Farm?" Aboard the last ship, still lacking female contact, a melancholy Scot walked the afterdeck, brought the wind into his bagpipes and gave forth with the ancient dancing tune, "Strip the Willow," then was hooted down and asked to be sensible.

McCoy, watching, listening aboard the *Arethusa*, felt a pleasant sensation of relaxation. This could do nobody harm, was in fact welcome. But then he remembered what he had learned earlier that same day. Geriard Haldenbach was dead. Haldenbach, one of the youngest, but the most daring and skillful, of the Jersey sea-skiff skippers had been killed by a stray Coast Guard bullet fired in warning.

Once, during the height of the winter gales, Haldenbach had ventured out alone in his skiff to the *Arethusa*. He came when the seas were so vast that McCoy was afraid to have him haul alongside the schooner; a single blow of collision would sink both craft. But Haldenbach insisted.

He was newly married, he had told McCoy in better weather, and he needed the money. Each lot of fifty cases he put on the beach was a neat three thousand dollars for him. Now he shouted over to McCoy that he could take his usual load. McCoy called back that Haldenbach was crazy, and to get the hell inshore.

Haldenbach hung on, however, and finally McCoy told the crew to give him the load. They held Haldenbach's skiff off with boathooks and oars as men swung far over the side and, with the lift of a wave, lowered a burlock into the cockpit. Fifty cases were aboard when a gigantic wave hurled down upon the skiff.

She was thrust sideways with its force, and up, and as the schooner took the wave's weight and rolled, the skiff veered onto her deck. But the next wave caught her, launched her from the still-awash deck and she was once more seaborne. Haldenbach shook the spindrift out of his eyes, waved as he pulled the throttle and headed for shore…

A stray bullet, McCoy told himself. Not fired in anger. But more would be fired, and with the angry intent to halt those who refused every warning to stop. The Coast Guard had new, much faster boats, seventy-five footers and thirty-sixes. Coast Guardsmen had been killed in brushes with bootleggers on the beach; shots had come from contact boats when ordered to stop. What had happened here today and tonight could only be a taunt to the patrol-craft crews. The fun was just about out of this. It was no longer what a thinking man could call a game.

Book Two

THE GO-THROUGH GUYS

CHAPTER SIX

While walking down Sauchiehall Street on a bonny day of rare Glasgow good weather, Alastair Moray was met by a chum who asked him if he wanted a job. Moray did. The Great Depression that had palled the British Isles during the early twenties was still being felt, and Moray was out of work. The job, his chum said as he took Moray into a public house for a glass of bitter, was slightly on the strange side, yet it would pay well. Moray listened and said that he was for it.

His chum sent him to a gloomy but neat office in a building occupied by certain shipping concerns. He was questioned there as to his background and, in particular, his sea experience. Moray said guardedly that the latter was somewhat limited; it was limited, in fact, to a few weekend sails in a small lugger yacht. Yet he was hired, at a surprisingly high wage, and out in the street again he realized that he was to assume the duties of supercargo aboard a ship that an Anglo-American combine proposed to send with a cargo of liquor to Rum Row, off the Port of New York.

Moray considered himself lucky. He was a man past thirty with intellectual inclinations, but also a liking for the footloose life and no strong family ties to hold him in Scotland. He took a bus for the Old Gavin Road, got off at the Clydeside dock, where the ship to which he was assigned was moored. She was, even to his marine ignorance, a disappointment. Her name was *Cask* and she was an iron-hulled schooner of bulky, clumsy lines, three-masted and obviously the object of a great deal of past mistreatment. Her overall length was considerably more than a hundred feet, he saw as he boarded her, with a deckhouse and a small bridge 'midships and a steam-donkey engine forward for the anchor.

The captain, bleary, a bit bellicose, met him at the cabin door. Moray showed his letter from the owners and was told to come in and sit down and have a mug of tea. Then the captain explained that the *Cask* was about ready for sea, with thirty-two thousand cases of assorted liquor, most of it Scotch whiskey, aboard. Moray would begin his duties as supercargo by checking the cargo and making a cargo tally, afterwards going ashore to buy a number of revolvers and rifles for the possible use of the crew on Rum Row. The captain spoke darkly of something more lethal that he had hidden aboard to dissuade any of them hard-case American gangsters who might try to rob the ship while she disposed of her cargo, and Moray surmised that he was in possession of a machine gun.

But Moray felt no particular fear of bloodshed on Rum Row; he had no personal information of the numerous fatalities caused by gangster attacks along the American coast. He checked the cargo happily enough and thoroughly, went ashore with money from the captain and bought the required weapons, gave them over, then sought his own gear.

The voyage promised to be of some months' duration. So he brought aboard with his clothing a number of books of poetry and a bagpipe. He was not yet fully master of the bagpipe, and he envisioned quiet nights at sea when he could walk the deck, skirling to his heart's content.

Her armament stowed, and the last of her fresh stores, *Cask* was ready to sail. The engineer wove his way below and the telegraph was tried on the bridge. The mate and the boatswain, neither of them quite sober, went to the bow and the donkey engine. Lines were cast off as the engineer roused an intermittent crepitation from his diesel, nursed it to give sufficient power to leave the dock. Moray stood on the short span of bridge with the captain and the pilot; he handled the engine-room telegraph at the pilot's orders and experienced a feeling of excitement. Glasgow lay drab, soot-dim astern, and ahead, down the windings of the Clyde, was the sea. Then France, Moray told himself. He had read the owners' orders with the captain. Then Rum Row and America, possibly a quick jog ashore to New York. It could be a fine voyage if all passed right, with a champion big piece of pay at the end of it.

The pilot having left the ship at the mouth of the river, the *Cask* hoisted her canvas off the Mull of Cantyre and headed down the Irish Sea. Most of the crew were still under the influence of the potions taken before sailing time, but even when fully sober, Moray realized, they would not make a reputation as smart sailors. It was well that he began to learn navigation and ship handling, and he closely watched the captain as the courses were laid off on the chart.

The *Cask* was bound for Le Havre first, there to enter into some legal stratagem with the French customs that had been invented by the owners and would satisfy British law as to her departure with such cargo. But right now Moray was interested in her performance under sail. That was miserable. She was sluggish before the wind, slow, cranky when hard on it. Her sails were badly cut, the booms rigged much too high, more wind missing them that caught them, and she was bald-headed, carried no topsails.

Cask was the correct name for her, Moray thought. She sailed like one, and in a bad seaway she would roll worse, give the contents of the cases in her holds a severe shaking. But she kept to her courses though the Irish Sea and St. George's Channel, put The Lizard astern and rounded up gradually towards the French coast.

Le Havre represented adventure for Moray. Here he was to have clandestine contact with the man known to him only as "The Boss," the head of operations for the combine that owned the ship. During the last day the schooner had been in Glasgow, a young assistant had been assigned to Moray, and Moray had already taken him into his confidence. The other man was an Australian, a former medical student who, for want of funds, had signed on aboard the *Cask*. Moray, of course, called him "Doc," and he and the rest of the crew were glad to have a man with medical knowledge as a shipmate.

Moray arranged that he and Doc go ashore together in Le Havre. They struggled with their French at a sidewalk café, dined, drank in style, then went back to check the cargo. It was being duly put on the dock, passed through French customs and immediately restowed aboard the *Cask*. The reason for such a complicated procedure, as Moray understood it, was the series of negotiations between Great Britain and the United States regarding contraband liquor. Washington had protested about the great number of vessels that plied their trade on Rum Row under the British flag. The two nations had agreed to extend the limit of American territorial waters three leagues, or an hour's good sailing time, out to sea. Washington wanted to dismay the contact boat crews, allow the Coast Guard patrol craft the opportunity to make pursuit. But, having been cleared through French customs, the *Cask* would, in the belief of her owner, be free from any violation of the British-American accord.

The reloaded cargo was tallied and the hatches shut. Then the *Cask* moved out from the dock to a remote anchorage. The Breton fog closed upon her and only a sailor on anchor watch was kept on deck. But, according to the instructions given him in Glasgow, Moray waited for the arrival of The Boss. A tug that made little sound appeared suddenly alongside, slid away again once her passenger had boarded the schooner. Moray greeted The Boss; they went to the chart table in the wheelhouse and Moray turned on the hooded light.

Two identical volumes of obscure French poetry bought ashore by The Boss were put upon the table. He and Moray studied them. They selected matching pages, phrases and words. The phrases and words were marked as the symbols of a code. Moray was to use them in his messages to the combine after the ship was on the American coast. Moray kept one volume, The Boss the other. The Boss looked at his watch, shook hands with Moray and wished him luck.

The tug was again quietly alongside. The Boss went aboard and a muffled bell rang in her engine room and she was gone. Moray walked forward to the bow of the *Cask*. The sailor on anchor watch slept, supported upright by the capstan. A good thing, Moray told himself. It increased the sense of mystery about this operation and strengthened his feeling of security.

The Boss had left sealed orders for the captain with Moray. The captain opened them in the morning in Moray's presence. He was not an exceptionally brilliant man, and was suffering somewhat from a hangover, a complaint that Moray had remarked was quite prevalent among the crew. Now he swore by the bloody ruddy that never in all his days of seagoing had he been given orders like these.

Where, he asked Moray, was any such flaming place as Rendezvous? Find it on the chart or in the pilot guide. Moray read the orders, translated the meaning of Rendezvous and pointed out that the captain was instructed to approach within eight miles of Ambrose Light Ship and there go to anchor.

The captain, so enlightened, put the transatlantic course on the chart and the *Cask* proceeded to sea. She picked up winter gales west of England, took weather that shook her until her masts bowed groaning, the crew's quarters were soaked and loosely stowed cases in the holds were shattered, permitting the crew to enter below and secrete bottles for personal stimulation from among the salvage.

Whiskey was mixed with champagne, topped off with dollops of brandy and green-mint liqueur. The cook, too drunk to function, locked himself in the galley against the probability of assault by the crew. But the crew, too drunk to care about food, stayed in the fo'c'sle and consumed their loot. The *Cask* sailed bare-poled waves higher than the bridge rail, the captain glumly incommunicative, the mate and the engineer and the boatswain stoical in their acceptance of storm as long as there was whiskey at hand.

Moray and Doc played whist in the soggy confines of the cabin. Delirium tremens, Doc made clear to Moray, would soon begin to wrack the crew, and from the standpoint of consumption alone, the boatswain would be among the first to suffer. When the weather diminished a bit and whiskey failed to dull the boatswain's brain, he was gripped by the horrors and staggered forth on deck from his cuddy.

He shouted with such intensity that the captain was disturbed, could no longer doze fitfully. The captain came onto the bridge and from that position of command confronted the boatswain and said he wanted to know what all the magenta row was about. Although the boatswain was sagging at the knees and sometimes toppled to the deck as he gesticulated, he replied that he was prepared to defeat the captain at fisticuffs. The captain told the boatswain not to be a bloomin' stupid goat.

This advice further infuriated the boatswain. He responded that the captain took undue advantage of him because of the captain's rank. He was, he said, just as good a gory sailor as the captain, if not an unmentionable amount better. Then, the captain held motionless by fury on the bridge, the boatswain started a lurid genealogical description. He went back to the captain's grandparents and placed them among the lower mammals, asserted that the captain's parents had been born far outside wedlock and had grossly cohabitated at the time of his birth.

The captain, choked with emotion, could only wave his arms and grimace at the boatswain. He stayed on the bridge, however, and his refusal to leave it emboldened the boatswain to a further flight of thought. Almost gently, he invited the captain down on deck for another reason than fisticuffs. He would explore with the captain a form of sexual expression related to that which had sent Oscar Wilde to prison. He and the captain would become lovers.

A howl came from the captain; he had broken through the barrier of rage and was in possession of both his voice and his rhetorical powers. He described the boatswain's own ancestry, going back to great grandparents whose obscene actions outmatched all known forms of depravity. He was dwelling upon the turpitude of the boatswain's grandparents when the crew stumbled from the fo'c'sle, bored by the monotony of drink alone, eager to breathe clean air, even to listen to the captain.

Some of the sallies amused them. They applauded. Then they started a ragged gavotte on the fore hatch, arms around each other's shoulders. The captain shouted at them to be silent; he was determined that the boatswain should hear him to the end. But the boatswain drooped. His posture became a hands-to-head sprawl on the deck. He made no response whatsoever when the captain accused him of being unable to tie up a bloody well perambulator to an effing park railing.

The crew had lost their pleasure in the dance. They felt the pangs of hunger. The cook's inactivity interested them and they told him through the galley door how they would change his physique unless he soon emerged with a full, and savory meal. The cook considered the proposition for a while and then opened the door and stepped on deck, not with food but with his largest cleaver.

Moray, watching the scene from a forward porthole in the cabin, formed the opinion that he should take his revolver, go forth and enforce peace. But in the last hour, huge thunderheads had gathered over the ship. Wind struck her swiftly, then a cold drenching rain; bursts of thunder gave a clangor that chased the cook back into the galley. Lightning rifted through the clouds. A green-blazing shaft descended upon the *Cask* and rippled downward from her mainmast truck.

Her iron hull was momentarily as active as a magnet. She glowed incandescent in the somber wastes of the storm. Sparks jumped from the galley stove; the coffee pot and frying pans nudged each other, chittering, and the cook screamed. The crew, ducked turtle-low, ran for the fo'c'sle. The boatswain, lifting his head, acknowledged the crack of doom, blinked in the glare and muttered that the captain was still a no-good sonofabitch.

The captain had taken refuge in the wheelhouse. Moray found him there. The captain was gasping with the effects of a severe shock. He indicated the wheelhouse compass wordlessly. The needle wavered through arcs of as much as 180 degrees. Moray and the captain climbed to the wheelhouse topside and the standard compass. That was knocked out, too, showed the same erratic behavior as the one below. "Don't know where we are," the captain muttered. "Can't get a position without these. Nothing for me to do. See you later. Need some sleep. You keep a sharp lookout."

Moray stayed for lonely hours on the bridge. He listened to the lessening force of the wind and the slowly sobering cries of the crew. The mate came up and relieved him near dawn and, with Doc, he went to the galley and cooked some food. Then, back on the bridge, he noticed that the compasses had begun to steady and hold approximate true north. He took navigation books from the shelf over the chart table, worked out the details of a Polaris sight.

Wind had frayed cloud from the sky overhead. He consulted with the mate then borrowed the captain's sextant. There was the horizon line, and the star he sought showed pale but clear as he adjusted the sextant and took his observation. The mate checked it for him, helped him plot it on the chart. They decided that the compasses were not too badly out, would eventually return to their correct headings. Moray, gratified and weary, went below, left the bridge to the mate. He was not a licensed man, he told himself, and he deserved his rest. Still, he shouldn't complain. He was lucky to be alive this dawn. It was quite a stroll from here to Sauchiehall Street.

The *Cask* thumped on west through a continuous series of storms, once more demagnetized and at best a sorry ship. The crew had drunk up all the whiskey they could filch for the time being; the boatswain had emerged to the perimeter of his horrors and performed small chores on deck; and the cook, seized without his cleaver, had been severely beaten and told to prepare decent food. The cook had been belabored past the point of culinary return, however. He sobbed over his pots that 'e' d 'ad enough, 'e 'ad. He slopped conglomerates onto the mess table in the fo'c'sle, and before the captain in the main cabin, that defied any digestion. When beaten anew by the crew, he only wept and sat huddled by the coal box in the galley, his tears dripping on his filthy hands.

A fine voyage, this, Moray told himself. It promised to lead to Poorhouse Alley instead of Rum Row and fortune. But the salt-whitened old schooner, with rust so thick on deck that it crunched under boot heels, caromed at last within sight of Rum Row. The captain could put the point of his dividers on the chart and say that this was Rendezvous and that, there, Ambrose Light Ship, and that on the skyline, New York.

The *Cask* took her place among her unkempt neighbors and Moray prepared for business. But for days there was none. It was the winter of 1923-24 and the weather was too rough to allow the contact boats to make their runs. The captain and the mate, bedeviled by anchor trouble, saw one insufficient cable chafe through its links, then another rip loose at a shackle. The *Cask* skated down the Row like a malevolent monster, barely missed a number of vessels and was at last fetched up with a backed headsail and the engineer's desperate manipulation of the diesel.

Moray was gaining more respect for the captain as a seaman. There was a break in the weather, too, and cargo could be sold. Moray put signs naming his brands and prices in the rigging and waited for customers. But first he and the captain had a talk and the collection of revolvers and rifles Moray had purchased in Glasgow was issued to the now-quite-sober crew. The captain passed an order: No craft of any sort except one belonging to the Coast Guard was to approach the *Cask* without being covered from the bridge.

While a sale was conducted and cargo transfer made, riflemen were to be constantly alert on the bridge and the crew members down on deck and in the holds were to have their revolvers handy.

The captain had picked up a considerable sum of information from his neighbors during the brief breaks in the rough weather. A new and grim term was in use on Rum Row—the "go-through guys." It applied to the vicious, merciless lot that had begun to prey upon the contraband fleet. The genesis of the term was in the fact that they were willing to go through, straight through any opposition for cash and kill to get it.

They were members of shoreside gangs or self-elected operators. They sailed fast launches that could outrun the Coast Guard with ease and overhaul most any contact boat. Hundreds of them roamed the waters from Block Island Sound to Montauk Point, Sandy Hook and Cape May. The targets they liked best were the contact boats. These, they sought just at dusk as the boats advanced from the coastal haven for the run to the fleet. It was the hour before the Coast Guard patrol craft were too close, before they began to pursue the contact boats; witnesses were scarce.

Moray had talked with some of the former contact boat crew members, chastened, defeated men who now chose to serve as deckhands at a regular wage aboard the vessels of the fleet rather than risk being robbed again or murdered by the go-through guys. From their descriptions, given with simple but realistic effect, Moray was able to visualize what had happened to them. He knew that he had been wrong in his estimate of the hazards to be confronted on the Row.

The go-through guys had a preference for the Thompson submachine gun, the stubby weapon that Al Capone had introduced into wide-scale Chicago gangster killing along with the automatic pistol, the ball bat, the ice pick and the dynamite bomb. It weighed only nine and three-quarter pounds, was thirty-two inches long. But it was .45 caliber and had a rate of fire of six hundred shots a minute. Operating the gun manually, by separate trigger pull, an expert could deliver from it one hundred shots a minute; and it was equipped with a Cutts compensator on the muzzle and magazines that took twenty, fifty or one hundred cartridges.

Against such a lethal menace the contact boats had small

protection. Their crews dared not arm themselves with similar weapons. If approached by the Coast Guard while running a load, the great majority of them made no effort to fight in order to escape capture. They would be arrested, brought into Federal Court, yes; they would lose their cargoes, and very probably their boats. But friends could put up bail for them; the usual penalty was a fine, at worst a year in jail. Then, with friendly assistance, a new boat was bought and they returned to the trade. They usually had no desire to kill or be killed, or to keep arms aboard. Coast Guardsmen, judges and juries were understandably tough with crews apprehended while armed. The fatalities among the Coast Guard personnel assigned to Rum Row duty grew almost each month.

When attacked by the go-through guys, the contact boats usually held crews of two, or no more than three, men. Their assailants numbered as many as six. The scene was repeatedly the same; the black-hulled boat with the pluming wake that connoted enormous engine speed. Then the inward sweep and the dark, crouched figures in the last of the sunlight. The Thompson gun was shown, the gunner straddled in the cockpit, his legs braced by a pair of his companions so that his aim would be precise.

The hail to stop came over the joined engine sounds. His boat rolling widely, the throttle down, the contact boat captain looked across at the men who were about to rob him. His hands were high; he had been told to put them there after he took his engine out of gear. But in his trousers pocket, bulging the cloth, was the roll of cash. Almost ten thousand dollars. He had intended to pick up 150 cases of whiskey tonight at the going price of sixty dollars, maybe load in a couple more of champagne.

He was told to pass it over, quick. His hand lowered slowly towards the pocket; the neat aperture of the Cutts compensator was on an exact line with his chest. During the final instant of hesitation he stared once more, his hatred nearly blinding, at the go-through guys. The gunner, the rest of them, wore fedora hats that the wind yanked, coats with flared lapels and low-cut, bright shoes. They seemed to dress in flagrant disregard of the forces of the sea. The contact boat captain and his crew wore cheap visored caps, woolen jackets and short seaboots. They were fishermen and all they had hoped for was a new dragger in the spring, or the mortgage off the house. Of course there'd been the hope, too, for a four door Nash, and if luck was real good, a Locomobile. Not now.

The roll was passed, hand to tense hand. But the Thompson gunner kept his stance. "Don't move, you guys." The black-hulled boat was gone then, surging to the power of her three engines, carving a marbled path over the shoulders of the sea, only her exhaust fumes a sign that a minute ago she had been there. The contact boat captain touched his throttle; he set it at half speed. Made no sense to head home fast when you were broke.

But sometimes, feeling a desperate anger, the boat crews fought back when ordered to surrender their money. A man reached for a long-handled wrench in the motor well, or tried to flip a fish knife out from under the deck coaming. There was never prolonged combat; amateurs were against professionals. The Thompson gun hacked, the cartridge explosions bunched in a rapid stammer. The bodies fell and were kicked aside by the go-through guys, who boarded to take the captain's roll, open the sea cocks or just put a burst of Thompson bullets through the boat's bottom planking, make sure she sank.

Out on the Row, the sounds of those murders were heard. Aboard the *Cask*, Moray could see through the binoculars the jagged stab of muzzle flame from the Thompson gun. He and the captain clenched the bridge rail, their fingers taut. Never two boats with big crews alongside at the same time, the captain of the *Cask* told Moray. And never more than one man from any boat aboard the schooner, and he must be the buyer with the cash.

Moray said that he understood. He told the captain that his orders from The Boss were to match pieces of a torn dollar bill with any prospective buyer who claimed to be from the combine. Then, too, he had the code pass words, and that should keep the *Cask* out of trouble.

The captain said that he still didn't feel entirely safe. There was the robbery of the *Mulhouse* they talked about here in the fleet, and all the Bahama-owned ships that had been boarded and pirated by the go-through gangs. A man had to keep a sharp lookout or he'd have his head banged fair off him. Moray agreed, said he would stand watch while the captain went below to try to eat what the cook stubbornly called supper.

Moray spent part of the watch in the wheelhouse. He entered in his diary the events of the day, even the language of his conversation with the captain. It was impossible, he wrote, to make any effort to practice the playing of the bagpipe or to enjoy his collection of poetry. But be could make a record of what went on along Rum Row, and the *Mulhouse* incident deserved its place.

July first of last year, according to witnesses who were reliable, had been a calm day, became a calm if slightly misty night. The *Mulhouse* lay motionless, light less at her anchor in the fleet. There had been some trade early in the evening, but now the crew slept. They were a French lot and the *Mulhouse* was under French registry, a shabby steamer of about one thousand tons, on which discipline was loose and the crew drank Scotch with their wine at meals.

Nobody was on deck aboard her, or awake, when the black schooner came alongside. Reports brought later from shore claimed that the schooner had sailed out of Sheepshead Bay and was commanded by the mysterious but very real go-through leader known as "Big Eddie." But those bits of information were no solace to the *Mulhouse* crew; the captain and his mates and engineers were cuffed from their bunks, invited within range of a Thompson gun to gather together with the others of the ship's company already under guard in the fo'c'sle. The invitation was very clear; the crew congregated in the fo'c'sle and the door to the deck was locked.

Then the ship was relieved of her cargo. But Big Eddie's gang did not hurry, and only part of the forty thousand cases of Scotch was put into the schooner and sent ashore. Eddie left a detachment of men aboard for three days, and they sailed boldly through the fleet in a launch and sold the remaining stuff for as little as seven and eight dollars a case. With the fleet market absolutely glutted, they set their course for the lights of Luna Park and disappeared. There was no alarm given, no chase made. Men from vessels around the *Mulhouse* freed her crew the next morning; her captain expressed some anxiety about how he would be received by her owners, but still hauled anchor and set his course for France.

The looting of the *Mulhouse* was the greatest go-through success on the Row as yet, Moray knew. But there were other stories for which he had definite substantiation. Three go-through guys working late at night and in silence had boarded a Bahama-owned vessel that had once been the property of Bill McCoy. She was the two-masted schooner *J. B. Young*, and had taken as cargo in Nassau a load of three thousand cases. The sleepy crew were locked in the fo'c'sle. The cases were sent ashore on the Jersey coast and the predators shared $180,000 as a cash prize.

Many men in the fleet suspected, however, that the *J. B. Young* piracy was not the work of a regular go-through gang. There were too many like it; with a quite systematic plan, almost every vessel that was under Bahamian ownership was raided. Their cargoes had been put aboard by liquor dealers in Nassau who had the expectancy of great additional profit if they were not forced to pay transportation costs to the Row. This attitude was resented by the crews of American-owned ships, and the American gangster combines that had been buying liquor in Nassau and using ships they controlled or owned considered it to be a grave encroachment upon the trade. Let the goddamn Conchs stick to their booze stores, not move in here, too, was the sentiment of the American faction. Each guy keep out of the other's way. What was this, a Limey picnic?

Dishonest dealing, treachery, robbery were becoming rampant on the Row. No man could trust another. With the approach of spring and the arrival of the contact boats in fair weather, Moray learned to be very wary. Sales started slowly, then increased, but his communications with the shore, despite the code he had devised with The Boss, were faulty, and he was convinced that some of the messages he received from the combine to deliver loads were counterfeit. The number of cases he was first ordered to turn over had been manifestly changed, and he was instructed to send them ashore without cash payment. He was also stuck with some counterfeit fifty-dollar bills by customers who simply appeared out of the darkness and said they wanted to buy.

The captain and the crew were of little help to him beyond the assistance they rendered in the physical transfer of the cargo. He kept his own accounts, decided who was to buy and who was not, and whether the money he squinted at under a flashlight, with the crew jostling him as they passed from holds to rail with the cases, was legitimate currency. When he checked the night's receipts against his tally sheet, he was profoundly fatigued, wished that he were back in Scotland even though he would be jobless.

The crew had undertaken a fresh round of debauch. They

detested the *Cask*, this work, this frustrated and lonely life. Here they were, cooped up on this rusty old bucket, and over yon, just an hour's sail away, was New York. They had hundreds of pounds in pay coming to them and not a farthing could they spend. The cook's efforts, important at any time to maintain crew morale, had degenerated into nightmarish concoctions that no man, no matter how hungry, would eat. The ship lacked a radio. Newspapers and magazines had not been brought out from shore by the combine boats in spite of Moray's reiterated demands. Cigarettes, pipe tobacco were nearly gone; the potato locker was empty, so were the vegetable bins. Card playing had been abandoned as senseless without a chance to take advantage of the winnings a man made. Women as a subject for discussion and nervous release had lost their appeal.

The crew drank and, part sober, got drunk again. Day by day the cook descended further into the ghastly caverns of delirium tremens and finally tried to kill himself, but was rescued at the last moment by Moray and Doc. The captain and the boatswain returned to their revilement of each other, but this, once mildly amusing, had become only filthy repetition. Moray retained his self-control by use of his diary. He recorded in it every fact of slight interest aboard the *Cask* and what he could discover about the rest of the fleet.

He made note of the fact that the beautiful white schooner *Tomoka*, which Bill McCoy still called by her former name of *Arethusa*, was again on the Row. She was famous, and Moray regarded her for long periods at a time through the binoculars. If there was any romance in this trade, McCoy was the man who had achieved it. McCoy had sailed on one voyage for the Row from Nassau with a strapping big dog aboard to guard the cabin and the cash. He had carried as his passenger on another voyage the slender, black-haired, gay woman who was known in the Bahamas as "Queen of the Bootleggers," and it was more than a title dreamed up by a space-hungry newspaper correspondent; it was justified in fact. Gertrude Lythgoe, an American citizen from California, had gone to Nassau in the very early Prohibition phase, set up her own wholesale liquor business in an office on Market Street. She had enjoyed herself hugely while McCoy's guest. He was a good host, and among rum-runners quite original in his evasion of the law.

McCoy had finally been trapped within the net of indictments intricately fashioned for him by Revenue Service agents. Just a few weeks before, in this spring of 1924, he had been arraigned in the Federal Court in New York City. His bail was put at fifteen thousand dollars, and the bondsman looked curious. McCoy carried a suitcase with him, and in it was sixty-eight thousand dollars in cash. He gave the bondsman the bail sum in neat packs of five thousand dollars apiece. Then, temporarily free, he skipped, left the jurisdiction of the court. The bail was forfeit, a tribute to the United States government in exchange for liberty, and by a route too devious for the Revenue Service agents to follow, he reboarded his schooner.

But McCoy was no longer insouciant. He was extremely conscious of the fact that conditions had changed on Rum Row. He had a tripod-mounted Lewis machine gun that he could put into almost instant action on the schooner's cabin topside. His crew were armed with rifles and pistols. He allowed it to be known through the fleet that a great deal of target practice had been held on the way north. Shark that had come within range in the Gulf Stream were speedily destroyed, and what could take care of shark would slacken any go-through gang's ambition to rob him.

McCoy had reason to be careful. A Norwegian-owned ship close alongside his in the fleet had recently been robbed. McCoy and his mate boarded her the morning after, and Moray also confirmed the story. The Norwegian vessel was ketch-rigged, had spent her best years in the North Sea fishing trade. Her owner was an old fisherman, gaunt, gentle spoken and not very bright. Tired of hauling herring, he had decided to make enough on Rum Row to keep himself and his family in retirement. He sailed from the United Kingdom with five hundred cases of Scotch whiskey, his son as cook, and a single deck hand. But he committed a grave error when, westbound, he shaped his course to call in at Nassau.

Some of the Lucerne Hotel gangster clientele made him a tempting offer. They would pay him three thousand dollars if he took one thousand cases to Rum Row for them. He accepted the charter, loaded, sailed. But on the Row, with most of the charter cargo already ashore, he began to doubt the integrity of his associates. He asked to be paid, at least in part, and his request was firm.

The ketch was raided that night. Men came over the side with pistols in their hands. The captain was knocked around, confined with his son and the deckhand. The go-through gang took off the remaining charter liquor and stripped the captain of his cash and all of his own Scotch except thirty cases that he had been canny enough to conceal beneath the cabin floor in the bilges. Before the gang left, their leader told the captain where he could go for his charter money.

The old Norwegian wept as he recited the story the next day. Tears rolled down his reddened nose. His mustache drooped wetly. He wore clumsy fisherman's clothing and long leather seaboots in the style of his native fjords. A lot of bastards, he said brokenly. Rob an old man, a boy, a deckhand. What kind of place, this Rum Row? It was no good, he said in answer to his own question. Then he shook himself, pinched together a fresh chew of snuff. The thirty cases of Scotch he had hung on to would bring in the cash to get him home. Back to the herring fleet. Better any time, and no crooks there, only honest fellers.

Moray, aboard the *Cask*, pondered the Norwegian's statement. He might feel much more secure about his own future if he rode some North Sea trawler instead of this semi-derelict with her alcoholically demented crew. Heavy squalls had demolished the last of the schooner's ground gear; she drifted to a makeshift anchor that the captain and the mate had rigged in a fit of despairing invention. Her working sails were ripped, flapped gray and tattered and defied the bosun's skill with a needle. The standing rigging was about to let go; turnbuckles were encased in rust; chain plates were relics of former strength; and no self-respecting rodent would go aloft up the ratlines. She must put into Bermuda or Halifax soon for major repairs. But the captain, lacking specific orders kept to his station on the Row. Provisions had finally been renewed from shore through the combine, and in the fair weather the crew took up al fresco cooking for themselves, ignoring the bumbling, incoherent inmate of the galley. Moray went on with his cargo discharge and his record of Rum Row events. The complicated procedure of theft and machination that now riddled the fleet fascinated him.

Double cross was superimposed upon already-complex double cross. Owners that did not trust their captains put agents whom they hoped were honest among the crews. Time and again, however, right after the last case was sold and the vessel was about to start homeward-bound, the captains took off with the cash receipts for the voyage. Supercargoes who were supposed to be the owners' sly but incorruptible men forged telegrams that instructed the captains to report ashore for further orders. Then the supercargoes, suitcases strapped tight over their cash contents, joined a fast-moving launch and were gone into the night. There were fake stickups by go-through gangs in which either captains or supercargoes held secret membership, and prearranged stickups which, when the cash was collected, proved not to be false, and the connivers were batted across the skull, left rueful aboard the robbed ships.

One captain, at the completion of weary months of anchorage on the Row while the cargo was sold, moved his ship near Montauk Point at the easterly end of Long Island. The vessel was in much the same shape as the *Cask*; she lacked supplies, even fuel for her engines and the galley stove. But the captain made up a tidy parcel of the receipts from the voyage, forgot any sense of responsibility and honor and was called for unheralded in the middle of the night by a lightless shore boat. The dilemma of the crew—they were provably rum-runners and the ship was well inside the twelve-mile limit—was solved by the Coast Guard. They surrendered themselves quietly; the ship was towed into New London and in jail they had their first good meal in weeks.

Moray, in his study of the machinations along the Row, was reminded of the problem of the absentee landlords in Scotland. There was a parallel between the two situations. In both cases, the owners generally were not present at the source of their profit. Space defeated them, and here in this fleet of nondescripts manned by disgruntled crews, they were fleeced worse than in Scotland, and very likely deserved to be.

But the Row, in the warmth, the light airs of summer, also showed a pleasant side. "Music," the seaplane pilot who was a Rum Row customer, was given competition. Other seaplanes in states of harum-scarum repair, their hulls sketchily caulked, put down beside the fleet on calm days. The pilots alternately pumped out and loaded whiskey. Maximum cargo for them was ten cases, and their destination, after dark, some inland Jersey lake or a marshy backwater near Atlantic City. The flight to the fleet was usually observed by the Coast Guard, however, and take-offs were hurried.

The maltreated old engines gulped and stuttered and the pilots stopped cursing and sprang from the propeller blur to grasp the controls. Then, like an osprey with a much-too-big fish, the planes tried to get off the water. They skittered, tossed spray and engine oil. The engines howled; struts vibrated between the flopping wings. A hail had come from the nearest Coast Guard craft. Warning shots were fired.

But the planes were airborne. As they climbed erratically, they no longer resembled osprey. Lunging across the sky to the west, they looked like awkward, outsize bees, stupefied by an overdose of nectar. Even the Coast Guard gun crews laughed at them. The shooting would stop at an order from the cutter's bridge. The trim white vessel would turn and steam austerely away down the Row.

The arrival and hasty departure of the contact boat *Rex* caused almost as great amusement, although the Coast Guard gunners felt no sense of sympathy for her crew. She and the *Sagitta*, a boat designed to meet the requirements of the original millionaire owner, were the first really high-powered craft to ply the Row. At the time they were both owned by a gangster combine, and the *Rex* was 65 feet over-all, had three Liberty motors that gave her 1,350 horsepower and a speed of close to 50 knots.

She came out early on a calm day and began to load, the crew contemptuous of any Coast Guard pursuit because of her speed. But they delayed, and the big cutter *Seminole* started towards her, the gun crew at battle stations on the foredeck. Cases were piled high in the *Rex*'s cockpit, a tarpaulin flung over them, and in his jump from the ship to the *Rex* one of her crew lost his handhold as the fast craft slammed off for shore.

His feet went higher than his head; he did a back somersault from the load into the turbulence of the wake. Three-inch shells that the *Seminole* fired bracketed the *Rex* and sent twin cascades over her. She was partly awash. Her crew bailed with tense haste; even a near miss could open her seams, throw her propeller shaft out of alignment, and she'd be an easy prize for the cutter.

But the man at the wheel was thinking of his pal in the water. He put the wheel hard over and set the throttle as wide as he could push it. Shimmering waves of spray flared from her bow. The magnificent triple-engine plant let go a roar that dulled the explosion of the *Seminole*'s shells. All through that part of Rum Row, crews scrambled into the rigging or onto the cabin topsides to watch the drama.

The *Rex* was cutting back in a full circle to make an attempt at rescue. The man in the water swam weakly; he had been hurt when he went overboard; his lungs were full of water from the tossing of the wake. But a pair of his pals aboard the *Rex* bent down for him. They grasped his arms as the boat hurtled past and he was yanked up, out, and then down into the cockpit.

The captain of the *Rex* did not spare another second. He eased the wheel, took her out of her radial swerve and steered her on a looping, evasive course for the Jersey shore that the *Seminole* could not intercept or keep within range. The Rum Row crews hooted in wild delight. They jeered the *Seminole* as she came about and at reduced speed went on in pursuit of slower, less daring craft.

But when the *Rex* made her next trip to the Row, the captain was questioned. Was the man he'd saved his brother? Did he figure to take such chances again if one of his crew fell over the side on a run? The captain laughed. "Hell, no," he said. "You think I want to lose my boat? But that guy was our buyer. The sono-fabitch was carrying forty-seven thousand bucks in his pants. It was worth the gamble."

Moray made note of that in his diary aboard the *Cask*. It gave light upon the peculiar form of Rum Row psychology: money was at the roots of any motive. But then his own ship was involved in an act of true mercy, and for some days he was too occupied to philosophize.

Fire had broken out in the engine room of a ship named *Alice*, which was at anchor near the *Cask*. Moray's assistant, the young Australian, Doc, had already been called upon to tend to various injured crew members in the fleet. His medical training informed him now that the burned engineer aboard the *Alice* would die unless given immediate hospitalization. Doc discussed the case with Moray and they agreed that it was difficult to solve.

If the injured engineer were taken ashore from the fleet, the men who accompanied him would violate American law, probably end up in prison. They possessed no papers of any sort that permitted them to land; they could not deny the fact that they were rum-runners, and while they might plead the necessity of their action, the Coast Guard or the Revenue Service might also welcome the chance to arrest them. But Moray advised Doc to go ahead, or the engineer would soon die.

Doc agreed. The second mate of the *Alice* volunteered to accompany him. A small launch was procured and the engineer, wrapped in blankets, gently handled, was lowered from the deck of the *Alice* into it. Doc and the second mate headed straight for Rockaway Inlet. They were not halted on the way in, but at the pier a curious crowd instantly gathered.

Doc and the second mate were bearded and bare foot, dressed only in dungarees and cotton shirts. But Doc climbed the pier ladder, talked to people in the crowd and then called the Rockaway Hospital. Before the ambulance arrived, Coast Guardsmen wearing sidearms had arrested Doc and the second mate. They admitted without quibble that they were aliens, had no right to be ashore, belonged to ships in the Rum Row fleet.

But the hospital intern who was in the ambulance assured them that the engineer would receive the best of care. Then they were marched off to confinement in the barracks of the Coast Guard station. The next day, early, they were brought into New York City for interrogation by both Coast Guard officers and Revenue agents at the Customs House.

They talked little and only in vague terms about their trade. Some vexation was shown at their failure to offer information, and the interrogation lasted several hours. Still, when it was finished, no charge was lodged against them. They were escorted by a high-ranking group composed of a Coast Guard captain, a Navy commander and an Army lieutenant and put aboard a Coast Guard picket boat at Pier One. The group did not leave them there, but sailed with them when they were taken out to the fleet.

Moray stood in amazement on the deck of the Cask as the boat drew alongside. He hastened to notify the captain, and the visitors were welcomed aboard. Food that came from the galley unspoiled by the cook's ministrations was served. This was tacit truce. Samples of the *Cask*'s various kinds of cargo were put upon the cabin table.

When the Coast Guard captain, as senior officer, indicated that his party must leave, everyone shook hands, expressed thanks. The final expression of good will was offered by the picket-boat coxswain; he tapped out a happy tattoo on the klaxon horn when clear from the *Cask*'s side and pointed for shore.

But the incident remained the only one of its sort for Moray. He never got closer to New York than the Row, and stared vainly at the towers which had become so familiar, yet were so far away. The captain of the *Cask* was at last forced by bad weather and the lack of working canvas to put into Bermuda. There were a few days of shoregoing in St. George's, and Moray made the most of them. He was delighted by the prim pink-and-white cottages, the dusty coral roads that led through vistas of cedars to the curving beaches, the frantic maneuvers of the American honeymoon couples on their bicycles. After the frowsy monotony of life in the fleet, Bermuda was very much next door to Paradise.

The *Cask* returned to the Row, banged at her anchor cable again, resounded with the shouts of her whiskey stupid crew. Moray had entered in his journal the events of 110 days' total service there when the order was finally received from The Boss to proceed to Halifax. It hadn't been anything like he had hoped, Moray told himself; yet, after what he had seen and recorded, he was lucky. His accounts came out reasonably straight; he hadn't accepted enough counterfeit money to put a dent in the combine's profits for the voyage.

He met The Boss in a hotel in Halifax, made his accounting. The Boss said that he had done quite well and that passage had been arranged for him on a homeward bound Cunarder. The crew of the *Cask*, The Boss pointed out, mistakenly thought that they were deserving of a bonus over and above their wages. They were not to get it, would sail the *Cask* home as their articles read, and would be wholly devoid of whiskey.

Moray took his gear off the *Cask* and waited impatiently for the Cunarder. But while he waited, he heard from Rum Row sailors just in from the fleet that Bill Mc Coy had recently stood trial in New York, been convicted of the charges he had accumulated and sent to prison.

McCoy had been the first of the really devil-may-care kind on the

Row, Moray knew, and the last. His day was gone. Now it was the turn of the go-through guys, the men who regarded murder as a logical part of profit-making. Let them have the trade and continue to betray and kill each other. Maybe, if they kept at that long enough, none of them would be left.

CHAPTER SEVEN

The theory of murder for profit in the go-through-guy manner had widened its appeal to the underworld mentality, and it became common practice in areas far beyond the Montauk-Cape May concentration of wealth on Rum Row. Coast Guardsmen, Revenue agents, local police patrolling the vast reaches of the Canadian border were shot down brutally, without warning, when they attempted to make arrests. Riddled bodies and half-awash, riddled boats were often found at dawn floating with the St. Lawrence current in the maze of channels around the Thousand Islands. Detroit, with its great bootleg market for hard liquor and the liking of a major segment of its population for Canadian ale, inspired a frightful scale of criminality.

Windsor, Ontario, right across the narrow Detroit River from the city, was the source of the illicit liquor supply. The usual hour of sortie for the rum running fleet from the Canadian shore was in mid-afternoon. Twenty or as many as twenty-five fast launches participated. They left openly, all at once, and they bore loads of scotch and French brandy, but even more Canadian Club, American rye, Labatt's and Black Horse ale.

The government was able to put an average of only two boats a day against them on the river, so that two rum-runners were captured regularly. But when those craft were sold at public auction, they were bought again by the gangs and returned to service. The scene during the chase had a serio-comic air; the boat crews about to be captured were really unconcerned.

Automobile ferries that had just taken aboard several hundred new cars at the Chrysler riverside plant would back out into the stream. Lanky ore ships, deep in loads from the Mesabi range, piled past for the down-lakes ports almost bow to stern in the heavy traffic. There were oil tankers and ships carrying steel scrap and tugs under tow, the United States Mail boat that here maintained a floating post office, the empty vessels upstream that kept in towards the Canadian shore, and a medley of small craft, some of them cruising casually, others, flying the burgee of the Detroit Yacht Club, interested as spectators in the rum-runner show.

The Coast Guard picket-boat crews and the men aboard the rum-runners knew each other because of frequent meetings. There was rarely a display of weapons, and the orders to halt were obeyed without protest. But the rest of the fleet, ducking in and out of the traffic, pulled in alongside the Detroit docks. Cars, trucks were ready. The stuff, in burlap sack lots, was unloaded, reloaded, and on its way. A block away from the river, in any open-doored speakeasy, the newly arrived ale sold for fifty cents a bottle; and throughout the city the bootleggers were busy at the adulteration of the other cargo before retail sale.

Fortune beckoned to the ruthless. The go-through-guy theory was popular. Legs Laman, hitherto a lackadaisical hoodlum, gained notoriety as a quick-trigger killer. He later adorned his criminal record with the kidnap of the Cass child, whose body was found in a gully near the Flint River. But his ferocity did not match that of Chet La Mare. A short and bull-necked man, swarthy, of Sicilian parentage, La Mare kept control of the depredations of the tough gangs from downriver. These were also Sicilian, and linked on an operating basis with the evil functions of the Unione Siciliana, allied in turn with the Mafia, which for more than a century had specialized in murder.

La Mare went on with his go-through tactics against other rum-runners until after the savage Fish Market massacre, when gangster shot down rival gangster. His fertile imagination had also taken him into what could be called legitimate business; he had the fruit-stand and lunch-wagon concessions at the Ford Motor Company; he was a co-partner in the Crescent Motor Sales Company, which handled the sale of Ford cars. But finally the hatred he had engendered brought death to him. He was shot in his own home, the police unable to identify the killer. The silver casket in which he was buried cost five thousand dollars and was the envy of local go-through-guy circles. It was carried to the cemetery, however, by professional pallbearers. None of his former colleagues would accept the honor, or risk the possibility of being blasted as they performed the rite.

Joe Tocco, who had worked for La Mare previously, was busy in the rum running trade and formed his own West Side gang after the death of his superior. He was killed at last in an ambush in 1938, and at The Brown House, a famous Dearborn establishment of prostitution frequented by gangsters, it was said that vengeance reached a long way. Tocco in his time had worked with Black Leo Cellura as well as Chet La Mare. But Black Leo had started his own East Side gang, and there was Tocco, looking for dough, too, with his West Side bunch of rum-runners. East Side, West Side. Try to go through both and cross up your old buddies and you came out like Tocco— dead. Some guys, they remembered a lot.

Along the California coast, in the fog-wreathed gap between the Farralones and San Francisco, there had been, since the inception of Prohibition, an occasional assembly of rum running ships that served the Bay Area trade. They were down from Vancouver and British Columbia and offered valuable liquor for sale. But the San Franciscans preferred to imbibe the local products, wine made by members of the Italian colony, rye whiskey which, if a bad imitation of the real article, was cheap. No temptation to accrue sudden wealth by treacherous violence was offered the criminal element when it watched the contact boats sidle in to discharge on a dark night at the Embarcadero or Fishermen's Wharf.

Further on south, off Los Angeles, much the same condition existed. There was nothing like the New York appetite to draw a large-sized rum fleet. Once in a while a sea-beaten old schooner tacked up the coast from Baja California, went to anchor off San Pedro, sent in agents with samples and got rid of a cargo. Still, the big spenders in the motion-picture business, the downtown sports and the patrons of the fifty-cents-a-slug speakeasies around Pershing Square depended upon the reliability of native manufacture or what came overland from Mexico in a slow but steady fashion.

The continental United States, except for the Rum Row zone off

New York and the Detroit River region, was free of the thrall of the go-through guys. They persisted in the Bahamas, however, and made the sprawling group of little coral cays, palmetto-ragged islands, sandspits and reefs their single overseas outpost.

Nassau, due to the maintenance by the insular government of a five-dollar-per-case revenue tax on all liquor that passed through His Majesty's customs, was in a state of financial stagnation after the first bonanza Prohibition years. A great many dark-hulled schooners still hung at the anchor off Salt Cay, but they were empty, the crews long since gone to other ships. The owners sat ashore ruminating about past profits, and stared at their silent warehouses or transferred their interests and gave up the trade.

Gertrude Lythgoe, with her bravura answers for any rum-runner's sally, had closed her office on Market Street. The Lucerne Hotel had a listless atmosphere; the bar did not quake at night with hoodlum shouts. Skulls were not broken, nor dice displayed, at the sight of a thousand-dollar bill. Invitations were not offered to step out into the alley and settle a dispute, Luger against Colt .45. Tommy, the barman, was bored. His present customers, in the language of the departed guests, were a collection of two-bit punks. A fire dance had not been held in the brush behind Grant's Town for months; a number of the Grant's Town belles had settled down into matrimony. Constables walked Bay Street at night undeterred by gangster challenges to knock them crazy or offers to turn that nice white helmet into a chamberpot.

By 1924, the Bahamian capital was again a town of memories. Jamaica, with no revenue tax on liquor in transit through the colony, had taken the business, and a great deal of it had gone, too, into the eager hands of wholesalers in Bermuda. Havana also supplied the Row with stocks of imported liquor and native rum, notably the Bacardi brand, which had growing popularity in the States. Pressure had released the restrictions in Nova Scotia and ships took aboard as much as forty-thousand cases at a time alongside the Halifax docks. St. Pierre and Miquelon were busy; they sent their own ships to the Row with French cargoes, sold at favorable prices to American and British customers.

Only the backwash of the original gangster tide remained in Nassau. They were a scummy lot, the former hangers-on who carried weapons but had never used them in a melee, who would inform on each other for the price of a drink and kick a constable after he had first been knocked down. Honesty was alien to their natures, and some few of them were daring enough to adopt the go-through-guy style of piracy.

The liquor trade that still existed in Nassau was between it and the Florida coast. It was marginal, did not interest big operators, and was conducted mainly in unseaworthy launches or old sponge schooners that took out a hundred or so cases and peddled them in the western most reaches of the Bahamas. These were the Bimini group, a loose-lying string of cays, with Bimini itself only thirty-eight miles from the American mainland. Bimini, with its cement-block Rod and Gun Club building, had been a smugglers' depot all along, and many thousands of cases had been stowed in its cellar while held for sale. Gun Cay, flat, gray-white coral and a few palmettos, was south of Bimini and another rendezvous point for the mainland contact boats. Cat Cay, further south, was the same.

The Bahamian schooner *William H. Albury* was in from Nassau with a load and at anchor in the limpid waters of Cat Cay when a pair of launches approached her. It was night; there had been recent robberies, and Captain Edgecomb was cautious. He was aboard the schooner with two other white men and a crew of Negro sailors, and he was not prepared to resist armed attack. He gave the order that the boat which had arrived first should get her cargo, only her men permitted on deck. Then he would deal with the second.

The second boat hung off from the side on her lines. She had three white men aboard her as crew and the man who announced himself as the buyer, Jimmy Truitt, was known to Edgecomb and his partners. Dawn came up while the first boat loaded. Truitt's crew cooked breakfast, sat talking quietly with each other. The loaded craft pushed off after payment had been made and Edgecomb invited Truitt aboard.

Truitt's crew boarded with him. All three of them went instantly into the schooner cabin. The two men there, Carey and Malone, had served as supercargoes in the deal just completed. Spread upon the table in front of them was twenty-one hundred dollars in small American bills. Truitt and his crew took out revolvers; Truitt picked up the money and put it in his pocket.

Captain Edgecomb was still out on deck, obviously nervous and suspicious. Truitt glanced at the captain through a cabin porthole. He told Edgecomb to come inside. When Edgecomb started to run along the deck towards the crew's quarters, Truitt shot him in the back. The captain spun around and fell dead.

Carey and Malone did not move from the cabin table. They were unarmed and Truitt's lot were quick to leave the schooner. The launch backed away, circled at top speed and headed for the Florida coast. When the schooner returned to Nassau and a report was made to the authorities, only a few more facts were learned. Truitt, in his haste to leave, had missed forty thousand dollars from sales that had been made before his arrival. He had sailed in a borrowed launch named the *Falcon* and the owner told the police that, along with seeing Truitt hanged, he would like to regain his property. But, things being what they were, he didn't expect either to happen. Truitt and his pals were gone into the wide blue American yonder, permanently.

While the authorities pondered the Cat Cay piracy, there was further news of extreme lawlessness in the colony. The settlement of West End on Great Bahama Island, well to the north of Nassau, had been invaded by a go-through gang. West End, originally no more than a few scraggly fishermen's huts, had gained great popularity and consequent wealth during the peak years of the rum running business. It was so situated in relation to the Florida coast that it became a very convenient liquor depot. Rum-runners who had loaded at Nassau and were bound for the Row also recognized the value of West End. They put in there to get clearance papers not quite as easily available in Nassau. These read that the masters of the vessels intended to make Halifax their port of cargo discharge. Halifax was, of course, a well-understood euphemism for Rum Row, but His Majesty's Collector of Customs took in his fees all the same.

West End prospered, grew rapidly wealthy. A palmetto-log dock substantial enough to bear the traffic was built. Warehouses were erected and filled to the sheet-tin roofs with a broad assortment of liquor. The population, less than a hundred formerly easygoing island Negroes, gave up fishing, sponging and turtle-catching as a livelihood. They handled the rum-runner cargoes, and they no longer went barefoot or considered salted codfish eyes a delicacy.

Shoes by the crate lot were imported from Nassau. Meat was on the tables at mealtime. American phonographs played American jazz for the workers' pleasure as they filed back and forth from the warehouses to the dock. Scotch whiskey was the favored drink, not shandy brandy, that product of the palm tree which, when distilled and drunk, battered a man into insensibility within the space of a few hours. Per capita, West End was the richest community of its kind anywhere in the Caribbean. Even with the decline of the Nassau commerce it held its place, supported by the Florida-bound boats.

Then the go-through guys arrived. There were three of them. They came alongside the dock in a slow-coughing launch, made fast and stood motionless for an instant while they surveyed the settlement. Only a schooner was at anchor offshore and she was not loading. The adult population slept, made love, listened to the latest Al Jolson record from Key West or read old copies of *The Nassau Guardian*. Children dawdled in the shade, and chickens chased lizards. The scene under the brilliant sun, with the azure, gleaming sea all around past the low island's spine, was beatific.

The go-through guys drew pistols. Side by side at first, and afterwards one to the right and one to the left, the third guarding them from the street, they began the thorough sack of West End. Everything that was of value and could be carried in the launch was seized. But cash, either American or British, was the real incentive of the raid. His Majesty's Collector of Customs was told to hand over what was in his possession. He pleaded the fact that it belonged to the government, pointed to the lion-and-unicorn seal over the doorway of his office. He was pitched into the street on his head and his small safe looted.

An air of efficiency was kept by the trio, although children screamed, women running for the shelter of palmettos reviled them and chickens got underfoot. The pirates wore neatly pressed shirts and hard-brimmed straw boaters; they seemed much more respectable than the rum-runner crews. West End was stunned. It was only the women who protested after the Customs Collector was thrown into the street; the men knew the deadly power of those pistols.

The sum of four thousand dollars in variegated cash, according to a later report, was taken from the citizens. Most of the other loot was discarded on the dock. But the go-through guys, although the raid had engaged less than half an hour of their time, went away angry. They were heard cursing each other as they put to sea in the launch. There was supposed to have been as much as one hundred thousand dollars here. The Customs Collector heard them and was seen to smile as he picked himself up from the street. He had sent almost the exact amount mentioned to Nassau only yesterday.

But the West End raid was not repeated. It was the single act of piracy of its kind during the Prohibition era. The Bahamas subsided back into torpor. One by one, urged by the Nassuavian police, the last of the Lucerne Hotel riffraff cleared out, and the place regained its stolid atmosphere. The hangers-on, however, were not ready to go to the mainland; gang activities there were too hazardous for men of their small degree of courage. They could live smart, they believed, and let others get killed trying for the big money.

Havana seemed to them to be a likely spot. Maybe in Cuba they could figure out the kind of deals that had paid off in Nassau. One of the endeavors in which they had taken part earlier was the transfer of American craft to British registry, with a cut given them for their ingenuity in the shenanigan. They would counsel a newly arrived schooner owner to get wise, play it safe. The scheme was this: the schooner owner bought locally several thousand dollars' worth of liquor. Then he told the dealer, a British subject, that he did not have the money to pay for it. The dealer put a libel upon the schooner; a few days later, the vessel was sold at public auction. The dealer made a bid that equalled the sum of the indebtedness and gained possession of the schooner. His purchase established her as British, and he at once sold her to the former owner, a fee going to him for his trouble, and another to the hanger-on who had brought the interested parties together. During the height of the Nassau trade, as many as five, sometimes six vessels a week were sold and resold, and always for a profit.

A further avoidance of the law had been devised by hangers-on who had sat for days at rear tables in the Lucerne before they could claim the attention of their more direct-minded companions. What, they argued, could any Coast Guardsman or Revenue agent do if a boat entered American territorial waters and the crew said she was in need of repairs? The reply to that was that nothing could be done; any craft in distress could demand the right to come into port. Sure, the Revenue Service would put seals on the cargo to keep anybody from tampering with it. But if the liquor aboard the boat was in wooden cases, not the burlap-wrapped lots? A little neat work with a finely ground chisel, a hammer and a pair of pliers at night could remove the nails from the cases and not leave a mark, and definitely not disturb the United States government seals.

The inventors of the idea gave a demonstration in the back yard of the Lucerne. They pulled nails, extracted imaginary bottles from an empty case, illustrated the fashion in which the nails might be replaced afterwards. Their suggestion was that suitcases would be the best means of transporting the liquor from the boat to the shore. Rocks or bricks, covered with newspaper, would lend the proper weight to the liquorless cases. If a real snoopy Revenue agent suspected that the cargo had been tampered with when the boat was ready to leave port and the crew asked for clearance, a fifty-dollar bill would act as a silencer, and for the more obdurate, a tap on the skull, perhaps a long walk off a short dock But those were details for the boat crew to decide. The idea could be made to work and should bring in a lot of dough. The scheme was used and proved successful; the hangers-on were credited for it; and some few of them were paid a share of the smuggled-cargo price because of their creative talent.

Havana, "the Pearl of the Antilles" in the language of its admirers, the oldest and the only city of any size throughout the Caribbean basin, should have been a haven for the brain-trust faction of the hangers-on who moved over to it from Nassau. It was cosmopolitan; people of many nationalities lived there. It was wealthy; even under the clamping, brutal dictatorship of Gerardo Machado most of the wealth was in foreign hands and was freely spent. Cruise ships from the States brought weekly crowds of tourists who sought to drink themselves silly, gamble with abandon at the casinos, keep the night clubs filled and the brothels busy. There was an active criminal population, well protected by graft, and a multitude of ways to live outside the law.

But in the malodorous Barrio Chino, where the outlaw element gathered, the hangers-on found little encouragement. Other idea men were ahead of them. French pimps who operated the international system which shipped women over the route from Europe that ended in Buenos Aires had taken occupancy of the Zanja Street bars. They used Havana as a drop, and their charges were next sent on to the cribs in Colon, then Bahia, Santos, Rio de Janeiro, Montevideo and the Argentine. They rested slick-haired and content, drinking *café solo* so black, so thick that it stained the sides of the small white cups. Their business was all arranged; they needed no reinforcement and they looked upon American gangsters as pistol-happy louts.

The Cuban rum running business was reserved for American combines that had regional franchises established on the mainland. A man could ride one of their boats and be paid a dollar a case for the liquor he put ashore, but that very probably meant being shot at by go-through guys along the coast. The groups which smuggled Chinese were highly secretive, intensely suspicious of any johnny-come-latelies who wished to join their numbers; a Federal agent might be among them. The Cubans, with the knowing surveillance of Machado's police, held as a prerogative the sale of counterfeit lottery tickets, pickpocket work, street robbery and the theft of property from drunken tourists.

The hangers-on were forced into the handling of dope, but they suffered no real pangs or moral scruples. Cube morphine was sold after delivery from Europe at ninety cents a gram. The price of cocaine was ten cents less a gram; the same amount of heroin cost the buyer a dollar, and granulated morphine was sixty cents a gram. All were popular smugglers' items. The drugs went out to the unfortunates of the American market aboard New York-bound ships that took home the tourists. Crew members who were often addicts themselves and poignantly in need of money hid the small packets inside hollowed-out shoe heels or in the lining of their clothing, and once aboard the narcotics were concealed within the steel stanchions of bunk frames, in fire extinguishers from which the fluid had been surreptitiously poured, in obscure crannies of the engine room, the forepeak and lazarettes.

Then, however, the capture of both sellers and passers became more frequent. Federal agents penetrated the Barrio Chino, and some aid was given them by the Cuban police. After a considerable number of arrests and deportations, the hangers-on desisted. This, too, was more dangerous than they liked. Back on the mainland the major go-through gangs were breaking up, killed off in internecine fights or trapped through vigorous law enforcement. Only one possibility remained for the riffraff—go home and try to turn honest.

There was a lull, and at the end of it, in 1927, a final manifestation of go-through savagery. This was of such an outrageous nature that the American public became aroused and no further crime of the same kind was ever committed. Prohibition was far from over; bootleggers were tolerated, even cultivated; Rum Row seemed to be an unchanging fixture of the sea approaches to New York, along with Ambrose and Scotland Light Ships. But bloody, unprovoked murder of government personnel must stop.

Bimini, in the western arc of the Bahamas, had remained through the years a flourishing center of trade for the rum-runners who served Florida. It was discovered, however, that counterfeit American bills had begun to appear among the sums put up for liquor purchase on the island. Chief Boatswain's Mate Sydney Sanderlin, attached to the Coast Guard station at Fort Lauderdale, was given orders to conduct Robert K. Webster to Bimini aboard the seven-man patrol craft, PB 249, that he commanded. Webster was a Secret Service agent and hoped to locate the plates and presses used to manufacture the counterfeits, and then, through British authorities, to apprehend the ring.

Sanderlin took his boat away from the Coast Guard station on a day of fine visibility. He knew the run before him very well, had often patrolled this thirty-eight-mile stretch of water between the Florida shore and Bimini. Standing with Webster in the pilothouse, his powerful binoculars raised, he recognized as suspicious the appearance of a launch that came over the horizon curve from seaward.

She lay low in the water for a boat of her type. Her rate of speed, too, made him believe that she was heavily loaded. It was not unlikely that she had taken on a liquor cargo at Bimini, was bound for some beach rendezvous near Fort Lauderdale.

Sanderlin shaped his course to pull alongside her. He called over to her crew of two men that she should stop. When she continued, Sanderlin set an ammunition drum in place on the Lewis gun he carried aboard, let go a burst that split the sea with a white furrow off her bow. She stopped.

Sanderlin sent men from his crew into the launch. She held in her cockpit 160 cases of whiskey. When questioned, the pair who sailed her said that their names were Alderman and Weech. Although these sounded as if they belonged to a vaudeville dance team, Sanderlin realized that he had caught professional rum-runners. He told them, "I've got to take you in. You'd better come aboard with me."

Alderman and Weech did not protest; Sanderlin still kept the muzzle of the gun out the pilothouse window. They boarded the patrol craft and Sanderlin ordered his crew to take the liquor from the launch. But then he remembered that he was supposed to make the run to Bimini and put Webster ashore there. His present orders did not include the apprehension of rum-runners.

Sanderlin was methodical, a career chief petty officer. He decided that he should get in touch with the station at Fort Lauderdale by radio. That was his fatal mistake, for as he tuned in the set and adjusted the head piece to bring in the station's signal, Alderman and Weech entered the pilothouse behind him.

An issue .45 Colt automatic pistol was on the chart table. Alderman picked it up, released the safety, put the blunt muzzle close against the back of Sanderlin's head and pulled the trigger. The chief died where he sat, his finger still on the sending key. Alderman stepped to the pilothouse door; he was committed and ready to kill again.

Machinist's Mate Victor Lamby had heard the shot on deck. He started to duck through the hatch into the fo'c'sle and procure a pistol. Alderman shot him through the spine, gave him a mortal wound. Then he told Webster and the other Coast Guardsmen, "All right, you guys. Take this stuff back where you got it." He brandished the pistol at the liquor cases stacked on the patrol craft deck and the men obeyed.

It was Alderman's intention to burn the Coast Guard boat. He sent Weech below to open up the gasoline lines, set the engine room afire. But Weech was a bungler. He told Alderman that he could not do it. Alderman sent him aboard the launch with instructions to start her motor, then stand by to shove off fast; he would take care of the patrol boat himself.

Weech fumbled when aboard the launch. He did not move quickly enough for Alderman. Alderman took his glance from Webster and the Coast Guardsmen and shouted to Weech to hurry. It was the instant for counter attack and it was taken; a concerted lunge was made for Alderman. He veered clear, kept erect for sufficient time to shoot Webster through the heart and immediately kill him, catch the boat's cook, Hollingsworth, with a burst of bullets that knocked the cook overboard, wounded in the shoulder and hand and blinded in one eye. But the survivors were then too close.

Alderman lost the pistol. He was stabbed by the galley ice pick, beaten across the face and head with a deck scraper. A strong man, he fought his way to his feet, was knocked down by further blows, kicked into unconsciousness. The Coast Guardsmen stood away from him and gave their attention to his partner.

Weech was still in a state of slow motion. Hearing the shots, the cries, the groans and blows, he suspected that something was wrong. He raised his head from the engine hatch of the launch. It was an excellent target for a boat hook dealt with a great deal of force. Weech reeled and was lifted by the shoulders and pitched over the side. When he crawled up and out on advice from the patrol boat deck, the point of the ice pick was put against his throat and he was made prisoner.

The *PB 249* returned to the Fort Lauderdale base with her dead and wounded and the launch in tow. Weech's courage matched his mental capacity; during the preliminary investigation he gave in, turned government witness and testified against Alderman. He saved his own life as a result, and Alderman stood trial alone for the three murders. Still, it was two years before Alderman was executed. There were court delays, pressures from various sources to have the sentence changed. But finally, with fitting, solemn ceremony, at the Fort Lauderdale Coast Guard base, Alderman was hanged until dead. He was the last of the go-through guys. With his death, they passed into history.

CG-100, the first of the 75-footers, of which 203 were built. *(U.S. Coast Guard Photo)*

Fleet of "six-bitters." Their job was to put an end to Rum Row by preventing contact with the shore. *(U.S. Coast Guard Photo)*

The 125-foot patrol boat *Tiger* stationed at New York. The class of vessels was known as the buck-and-a-quarters. *(U.S. Coast Guard Photo)*

Crewmen from the USS *Ericsson - C.G.* The destroyer was stationed at New London, Connecticut. *(U.S. Coast Guard Photo)*

Admiral Frederic C. Billard, Commandant of the U.S. Coast Guard from 1924 to 1931. Billard died in office. *(U.S. Coast Guard Photo)*

The *Tucker* and the *Cassin*, two of the 36 ex-Navy destroyers taken over by the Coast Guard for use in Prohibition enforcement. *(U.S. Coast Guard Photo)*

The *Tucker* was the flagship of the destroyer force at New London, Connecticut. *(U.S. Coast Guard Photo)*

Book Three

THE COAST GUARD

CHAPTER EIGHT

Throughout all the Prohibition years, until and even after Repeal, the Coast Guard played an unhappy role that gained it a vast amount of notoriety it did not really deserve. The first of our seagoing services, small and yet justifiably proud, it was suddenly thrust between the public and the new class of lawbreakers which Prohibition had made wealthy and powerful. The Coast Guard, ordered to carry out an unpopular law, was harassed by resourceful criminals both at sea and ashore and also, often grossly corrupted enforcement officials.

President John Calvin Coolidge, in his Annual Message to the Congress at the end of 1923, promised that the Coast Guard would soon be strengthened. Rear Admiral F. C. Billard, the Coast Guard commandant, had estimated that his force needed an appropriation of $28,500,000 for the correct performance of its added duties. This sum embodied the cost of 20 new cutters, 203 cabin-cruiser launches of the 75-foot class, 91 smaller patrol craft and the enlistment of 3,535 extra men for them. Congress debated the President's request and in April, 1924, appropriated $13,000,000 for Coast Guard use, an economy having been achieved by the transfer of twenty World War I destroyers from the layup fleet. These were vessels with high superstructures and narrow hulls that, according to the crews which had manned them in war time, rolled their beam ends under when at anchor on a calm day in a backwater. They were known colloquially as "four-pipers" because of their array of tall, thin smoke stacks; they burned coal in an age of oil and spread wide banners of smoke astern when under weigh, and at night belched sparks that a sharp-eyed observer on Rum Row could see for miles.

But the Coast Guard was happy to get them. Captain W. V. E. Jacobs, in command of the New York Coast Guard District, in 1924 was able to report that within three months after they had gone on duty, ten million dollars in liquor and boats, a careful appraisal, had been seized. Rum Row found it wise to move out to sea temporarily, in the hope that such interference would stop.

The fleet gathered again in the same general area. There were now, among the contestants for the market, vessels from the United Kingdom, France, Norway, Italy and Costa Rica, as well as their American sisters. All of these loaded in Bermuda, Havana, Belize, Halifax, St. Pierre and Miquelon. Foreign-flag captains were very angry. They didn't like to be pushed around so, they told each other as they visited ship. It hurt business, and, by Joe, it wasn't even legal.

Observance of the twelve-mile limit, legal outgrowth of the Eighteenth Amendment, was in dispute. The foreign-flag owners and captains argued the ancient right of freedom of the seas. American law said that they should keep beyond four leagues from shore, and that was interpreted by the Coast Guard as twelve miles, equivalent to an hour's steaming time out of a coastal port. Boarding and seizure were illegal past the twelve-mile distance, the foreign-flag people insisted, yet they preferred to remain outside that and were still wary of Coast Guard approach.

The primary purpose of the Coast Guard was to render impossible the contact boat traffic to and from the shore. The patrol craft crews were ordered to be stringent with any such boats, seize them, their cargoes and crews, bring them in, break up the trade. The farther out the Row was driven, the easier the task of capture and the greater the danger from weather conditions for the smugglers. In effect, a coastal-blockade system was established. The Coast Guard had without qualification the right of seizure of American-flag vessels anywhere in the world outside foreign territorial limits. When the smugglers plying the Row off New York became reluctant to try a run a number of the liquor-carrying ships shifted a bit to the northward.

The maneuver was made to penetrate Long Island Sound, and to put cargoes ashore in Connecticut and Rhode Island. Laden contact boats whipped in at night around the dark loom of Block Island, ran the tide-rough waters of The Race, then ducked down the Sound or crossed to Saybrook, Stonington, New London and the beaches below Watch Hill. A countermaneuver was made by the Coast Guard. Local headquarters at New London set up a double patrol screen. Well out to sea, clear of Block Island and Montauk, the cutters and four-pipe destroyers maintained station. Off The Race and inside Long Island Sound were the seventy-five-foot craft, and right in along shore, working in close cooperation by radio, were the thirty-eight-foot picket boats, whose crews communicated in turn with the beach patrols and the mobile truck units. The smuggling trade was steadily, stubbornly diminished.

Yet it persisted. There was too much profit involved. Faster and more seaworthy boats were built and sent to the Row. Crews took greater chances, and behind them, ready to pay their fines, engage lawyers with strong political connections and rehire the crews if they were unfortunate enough to be sentenced to jail, were the big gangs, the combines that had begun to take over every phase of the illicit-liquor business. Admiral Billard, who had reported in 1925 to Secretary of the Treasury Andrew W. Mellon that Rum Row had been "effectively scattered," was forced to admit that increased measures should be taken against it.

The extent of the tactical problem was manifest when twelve Coast Guard craft were assigned to cover the area between Gay Head on Martha's Vineyard and Montauk Point; the distance between the landmarks was well over sixty miles. The cutters and the ex-Navy four-pipers kept plenty of sea room and most of the time maintained vigilance over the Rum Row ships. The seventy-five-footers, known as "six-bitters" in the service, aided them, and while on the duty each seventy-five-footer was ordered to watch a particular ship, stay with her no matter what the weather or the ruse she might attempt. When she started to discharge into the contact boats the Coast Guard moved in to arrest and make seizure.

It was a nerve-wracking, difficult and dangerous job. All of the Coast Guard craft ran completely blacked out. Fear of collision was constant in the mind of any man on watch. These were thickly traveled waters. Commercial fishermen worked them; coastal tankers, colliers and passenger vessels traversed the area; deep-sea ships were bound into or out of the Cape Cod Canal; in the summer, hundreds of yachts sailed between the islands and the mainland, and some of them maintained a poor lookout after darkness, even resented the presence of the Coast Guard. There were fogs, snow gales, weeks of drenching, blinding rain, and at expiration of a tour of duty, when the patrol crews were ashore, they found that they were alternately called "gun-handy" by the Wets, and referred to in newspapers as "Carrie Nation's Navy," or criticized by the Drys for failure to stop the smuggling traffic within the current year.

But the Coast Guard, although a number of men on the musters became disheartened and disaffected, accepting graft from individual rum-runners, the gangs or the combines, took a determined attitude. This was a challenge for sailors. The rum-runners were increasingly wily; the ruses were met by equal guile, keen vigilance and smart seamanship.

The destroyer *Hiram Paulding* had a powerful, long-range searchlight installed right on her bow. The officer of the deck had no more to do than stand behind it and keep its rays trained squarely on the stern of the rum-runner that navigated in wild parabolas to escape. Another destroyer, the *Jouett*, on the same Gay Head-Montauk Point duty as the *Paulding*, received, when in at dock, what was to be her captain's most valued possession. It was a searchlight with a sixty-inch lens, and the captain had it mounted on the wheelhouse topside. He lay alongside it many a night through, stretched out in a rubber doughnut raft, protected by a blanket and warmed by cups of coffee provided by the watch. He turned the switch at the correct instant and the giant beam cut across the sea, limned in full silhouette the Rum Row ships on the horizon.

Patrol-craft crews learned to recognize which contact boats were decoys, sent to lure them off station while the flotilla with the load spurted through the gap. Luminous tracer bullets were used invariably in night pursuit. A series of bursts from a Lewis gun in the hands of a chief boatswain's mate, firing at a contact boat, gave him at least a fair idea of her position and was also a signal to the other Coast Guard craft, warned the sentries on the beaches. They were persuasive, too, as a deterrent, and if not, a shell from the one-pounder cannon that the seventy-five-footers mounted on the foredeck was sent over the eluding boats' bow.

Still, the seventy-five-footers and the thirty-eight-foot launches that worked farther inshore were at a severe disadvantage while in chase. Many of the contact boats owned by the combines were built in the yards where Coast Guard contracts had been let. The combine agents waited only long enough to discover the exact speed of the new Coast Guard craft. Then they changed their contracts, made certain that their boats would have an additional knot of power to pull them clear from capture. Coast Guardsmen on duty in the Lower Bay of New York Harbor were dismayed by an exhibition put on for their benefit, and word of it spread through the service.

A new contact boat had just come from a Brooklyn yard, been commissioned and was ready for her trial run. It was a sunny day with fine visibility and at slack water the *Ile de France* proceeded outward bound down Ambrose Channel with the intention of breaking the transatlantic speed record. The great French passenger liner tossed a bow wash high as she surged for sea. She operated with her engines at their maximum rates. Then the contact boat whipped along the channel after her.

The man at the wheel set his craft into the wake of the *Ile de France*. He waltzed her out of it and then sent her around and around the liner in pirouettes that reached a speed of fifty knots. The captain, the staff captain and the pilot looked down amazed from the *Ile de France* bridge. The coxswain of the contact boat waved and smiled. But the Coast Guardsmen on harbor duty did not wave back as he passed them. This was hard to take; out on the Row, the patrol crews would be beaten before they started.

The patrol crews found several things hard to take. While they were allowed to proceed blacked out at night, the law forced them to prove identity before they made a capture. The small hand flashlights that, up to now, had been used only in the pilothouse for a quick look at the chart or a stubborn ammunition drum were aimed upward at the Coast Guard ensign on the halyards. Then, the pursuit legal, the order was given to the contact boat men to surrender.

Many smugglers, aware that they were about to be arrested, employed the classic tactic and tossed the evidence over the side.

Better an empty boat than a year or two in the Federal penitentiary in Atlanta. There was also tomorrow night and a chance at another run. They sat in the boat and mildly cursed the Coast Guard; they were honest fishermen. Look at the handlines, the cans of bait.

The Coast Guard in most cases sheered off without much exchange of dialogue. For if they lay drifting here and argued, other rum-runners would see the display of light upon the ensign, take a fresh set of bearings and start for the shore. And if the Coast Guardsmen brought this lot in, there was no charge that they could make stick against them. Just as often as not, the law was with the rum-runners. There had been enough cases in which, during a chase on a dark night, a rum-runner had been wounded; later, in court, fast-talking lawyers had shown juries that the boats were empty, carried no contraband at the time of arrest. So, very logically, the Coast Guard—not these falsely accused men—was guilty.

Patrol crews, over a hundred in each of the big vessels and seven in the seventy-five-footers, spent thirty days at sea and then were given ten days of liberty in port. Boredom infected them, and the ten days were all too short. Men talked only of getting out of the service.

They counted, recounted the time yet to be put in before they could ask for discharge. Even the old-timers, the professional petty officers and chiefs who had looked forward to a long career, lost interest in the service.

Aboard one seventy-five-footer that for weary months had been on Rum Row duty, the crew slid into a mood of sullen abandon. They had been promised relief for Thanksgiving liberty and it did not come; the relieving craft was delayed. They had been promised Christmas liberty, and again they were not relieved. Some dunnage planks were piled on the afterdeck. Long-shanked eight-penny nails were in the dunnage and those were pulled out with the knowledge of the old-time chief who was the captain of the boat.

Salute charges were taken from the ammunition locker and ranged beside the one-pounder cannon on the foredeck. Men among the crew said that they were real expert at duck shooting; let them handle the piece. A salute charge was introduced into the breech of the cannon. Nails by the hundreds were poured down the barrel. The boat got under weigh with the chief at the wheel and across the dismal winter sea ducks were sighted. The chief pursued, slowing down the engine so that the ducks would not be disturbed and the volunteer gunners might aim with accuracy.

But at the last moment the chief desisted. He had a clear idea of what the nails would do to the rifling of the one-pounder. But the crew prevailed upon him, and in the small confines of the boat he could not avoid them. A watch cap was passed; a collection was made. Then the chief steered the boat in alongside an isolated Rum Row ship and liquor was purchased.

The chief and all hands got very drunk. With partial revival, the duck hunt was again discussed. The chief was ready to agree. No Thanksgiving dinner, no Christmas. Let them eat duck, by God.

They chased the flights with some alacrity, but the gunners were not wholly certain of their aim. Great showers of nails ripped forth from the muzzle of the one-pounder until the cook said that he had sufficient fowl for a meal. The nails, he pointed out, were a little bit heavy for the job. Most of the birds scooped aboard were so battered that he would have difficulty in plucking them. Then there were all the nails to consider; a man didn't want to chew on them. He wanted to eat duck.

The crew ate, sobered up and returned to duty. But the relieving craft brought an officer who inspected the boat. He opened the one-pounder breech in routine fashion to examine it and noticed an absence of rifling. He went around to the muzzle, trained the gun towards the sun and studied it thoroughly. Then he went to talk alone with the chief in the pilothouse.

The chief unhesitatingly explained the circumstance. He and the officer sat for a moment in silence. The officer said that if he didn't do it, the next officer to come aboard for inspection would. The chief answered that he understood. He made a brushing motion which indicated that the eagle above his chevrons had taken wing. He repeated the gesture over the re-enlistment stripes on his sleeve. The chief was through, finished with the Coast Guard, pension hopes and all. Any court-martial before which he stood trial would find him guilty.

In port, his shipmates said goodbye to him with affection. They wished they were going with him. To hell with this stuff. No more Rum Row for them. They'd go to the shore stations or on beach patrol as soon as they could draw their transfers.

CHAPTER NINE

The shore-patrol units in themselves, however, were convinced they had a difficult duty to perform. The stations they served stretched along the seaboards of the Atlantic, the Gulf and the Pacific from border to border, but in the Prohibition era the main concentration was, of course, on the Atlantic coast between Cape Ann, Massachusetts, and Cape May, and the Long Island shore in particular.

Chief boatswain's mates, the career men, the sea-wise veterans, were in command of the stations. They had ten men under them as a rule, and, practically without exception, these were "boots," green recruits serving out first enlistments. The station crews lived well enough, if simply, in regulation barracks on ample rations. But their pay, balanced against the amount of bribe money offered them by the smugglers' combines for malfeasance, was ridiculous. The lowest Coast Guard rating, surfman, got $60 a month, plus 75 cents per day subsistence, whether married or unmarried. A boatswain's mate second class drew $72 a month, and a chief boatswain's mate $126, and none of the hands received an increase in their base pay during the first enlistment period of four years. Afterwards they got 10 percent over basic pay, then 15 percent during the next four years, and, with twenty years in, were paid 25 percent more.

The greatest temptations were offered the chiefs. It was they who could very easily divert the patrol movements of an entire station area, let pass enormous cargoes of liquor in the space of a night. Many did succumb; some were caught and given dishonorable discharges from the service. Not a few became bootleggers or rum-runners' agents, using their knowledge of Coast Guard tactics and frequenting the local pool halls, bowling alleys and restaurants where their former shipmates came for relaxation when on liberty.

Transfers from station to station were frequent, in order to break up attempted or actual collusion. On March 6, 1925, for example, District Superintendent Simon R. Sands shifted around his units on the South Shore of Long Island, reassigned men at Point Lookout, Short Beach and Fire Island to decrease the incursions from Rum Row. The complex of coves and inlets surrounding Fire Island formed a very favorable landing zone for the smugglers; successful pursuit there on a dark, foggy night was almost impossible.

Farther up the South Shore, on towards Montauk Point, the station crews were kept extremely busy. These men patrolled from Ditch Plains, Amagansett, Napeague, Georgica, Hither Hills and Mecox. Breakers from the open Atlantic came in upon the beaches they marched. The men carried no weapons, were armed only with Very rocket pistols to summon their mates in the event of a landing attempt.

It was lonely work, and in foul weather, wretched. Men stumped along over the dune grass and at the edge of the combers in seaboots and oilskins and sou'westers, heads down, sweater collars up, shoulders hunched to the weather and eyes squinted against spindrift. The foot patrols were turned out at four in the morning and kept going until six. The watches were of four-hour duration, but when visibility was poor, they were limited to two, and from March twenty-first to September twenty-first the dawn patrols were eliminated.

Fair weather or foul, a watch was always maintained in the diagonal lookout towers constructed at each station. The man on duty aloft in the tower was able to see the boundaries of the zone allocated to his outfit, and through binoculars he scrutinized the progress of the foot-sloggers, the seascape which suddenly might be decorated by a laden contact boat, and the dunes behind which the trucks and cars of the New York convoy would wait until ready. He was allowed to smoke while on duty in the tower, but not to sit down or show a light; and at hand was a telephone connected with the station switchboard and the phones in shacks at each end of the zone where the foot-sloggers halted. The foot-sloggers punched time clocks each half hour, and after their beach duty were relieved, went up into the tower for the rest of the watch. The tower men then went on beach duty and strode the three and a half miles east, the three and a half miles west that was the extent of their patrol. All patrols walked in the same direction, either east or west, so there was no duplication of effort and no overlap of sentries.

During the depression that followed World War I, the Coast Guard in its expansion program, had enlisted a good number of Southerners. They were mostly boys just out of their 'teens from the red-clay Georgia hills, the turpentine-pine country of North Carolina, and the tobacco farms and small, isolated towns of South Carolina. Seagoing was not in their blood. What seemed to them to be a beneficent government had given them the chance for regular food and pay, even a chance for advancement if they learned to read real good. The chiefs who were over them were men from another tradition.

The chiefs were New Englanders—State of Maine men, Massachusetts men, Rhode Islanders—and from Jersey and the maritime counties of Virginia. A good part of them had seen sea duty in the war. Among the lot, too, were veterans of the old Lighthouse and Revenue services, and these were sailors who could splice rope in the dark, tell the wind direction and velocity while lying in their bunks. They were happiest when handling a surfboat at rescue work in a flourishing nor'easter, and they had a natural disdain for their subordinates.

These kids couldn't make a hold-fast knot when standing on a sunlit dock on a windless day. They walked as if shoes hurt their feet; telephones were still mysterious instruments to them and they had the tendency to keep their quarters in a pig-sty style, treat their uniforms and all their gear without pride or concern. The chiefs did their best to make sailors out of them, and in some cases succeeded. But they lived apart in spirit from the rest of the station personnel. When they went on liberty, it was with a vast feeling of relief.

The chiefs were men who, because of their calling, did not look with disfavor upon alcohol as a beverage. There were speakeasies in the small towns they visited or where their wives and families lived. Real sailors, fishermen, Navy veterans, men who had sailed in the deep sea merchant marine and in the menhaden bunker boats, frequented the speakeasies. Drinks were bought back and forth; stories of the old days were exchanged. Then a hundred-dollar bill, sometimes a five-hundred or a thousand, was slipped beside the chief's glass on the bar. A former Coast Guardsman, an ex-chief in a costly civilian suit, with a new Marmon or Pierce Arrow outside in the street, was often present to see that full protocol was observed.

Another round of drinks was bought. The chief from the local station was told quietly that he should pick up the money. Look, what the hell was going on in New York? How about the graft in Washington? A man was stupid to knock himself out for a chief's lousy pay when in a month he could make enough running booze to buy a house, a car, put money in the bank that would send his kids through college. If he didn't want the money, leave it, and no bad feelings. He'd still be stupid, though, and he might get his head shot loose down on the beach some night.

Many chiefs applied for sea duty just so that they might retain their integrity or avoid being caught in some connivance of which they held no prior knowledge. Others left the service at the end of an enlistment, joined openly with the smugglers and became a part of the shoreside operation. A further number stayed on in the service, accepted graft, allowed liquor cargoes to be landed and sent to market and, when accused by their superiors, stood court-martial trial, were discharged as unfit. There were enough severances to deplete the ranks of chief petty officers; examinations were held often for enlisted men who sought to qualify as chiefs or looked forward to the pay and privileges of warrant officers.

Beach-patrol vigilance suffered. Young surfmen slogging over the dunes no longer paid particular heed to what went on around them. They stared casually out at the buoys that marked the channels, the reefs, the shoals. Behind them, lifting high, then swerving in a great scythe-like arc, the Fire Island Light Ship beam crossed the sky through its vector. Ahead, dim with distance, Montauk Point Light sent a similar beam that here was only an ocher blur in reflection upon cloud. Planks from the wreckage of a beam trawler chaffered in the undertow along tide mark. The wind made a minor yet insistent hum in the crab grass along the dunes. Farther back, among the stunted pines and the berry bushes, a pair of cock pheasants met, aroused by dawn, and fought each other with a hirruu-hirruu sound, the flap and smack of wings. A young buck deer was startled; he broke from the bushes and stood for an instant nervously alert on a dune crest, the rack projected forward dandy against the dawn radiance now lifting from the sea horizon. Then, in a single leap, the buck was gone, the hoofs like a drum beat, the legs, the body raised so that the bay-berries were only knocked softly to the ground. A rabbit squealed, and the Coast Guardsman knew that a house cat left last fall by some city folks had pounced, seized it by the nape.

The Coast Guardsman was weary and hungry. In his imagination he could smell the coffee in the big zinc urn in the station galley. There was the smell of ham and eggs, too, and buttered toast, cig-arette smoke that he had inhaled deeply. Imagination took him fur-ther; he was home in his North Carolina town and across the square from the porch of the store where he stood was the skinny blonde he liked. She wasn't too skinny for him, and after he'd bought her a Coke or two they'd go for a walk down along the crick where the pine trees grew big and there was a thick spread of needles like a carpet underfoot.

He shifted the weight of the time clock and the Very pistol on his belt. His legs were stiff from marching. Sand was in his shoes; he would take that out when he sat down in the shack up there at the boundary. Then, after the clock was punched, he would start back, and this was the last piece of the watch. But off there, just outside the red blinker buoy that broke for two and a half seconds and showed the inboard-channel turn, was a boat. No lights. Damn lit-tle noise with that underwater exhaust. And riding low as she crossed the bar and came in past the blinker. That was a rummy.

The Coast Guardsman went into the shack. He took the phone from the cradle, then put it back. Men were on the dune crest where the buck had stood. He could see them through the door-way of the shack, but, still in darkness, he was unseen. Ring the phone, talk out to the switchboard at the station and they would hear him. He stood motionless.

The men were moving down from the dune. They went in dou-ble file to the boat beached at the head of the inlet. When they turned and came back up, they bent under the weight of a whiskey case on each shoulder. But they walked fast, and over the dune the

Coast Guardsman heard now the motors in the trucks and cars. He waited in the shack, rigid and very quiet against the wall.

When the convoy had left, muttering in low gear through the dunes and roaring on the highway, and the boat was back at sea beyond the channel, the Coast Guardsman stepped from the shack. His chest was congested with strain; he coughed as he lit a cigarette. But no sense to get killed, he told himself. He didn't have a gun. And back at the station the new chief wouldn't care about the load that had just gone through. So don't say anything. Next time he had a piece of liberty, though, he could mention it to the right folks over in the speakeasy in the village. Might as well go home and buy that skinny gal a dress she'd be proud to wear.

CHAPTER TEN

Alongshore, running the coves and inlets and estuaries which for many of the smugglers had been family sailing grounds for generations, the Coast Guard sought to hold within the law a formidable group. A reporter for the *New York World*, while at work on a Rum Row story on the New Jersey coast in July, 1927, prodded the officials of Cape May City into the exhumation of old records which showed that illegal-liquor traffic had existed locally as early as 1692. The officials made the distinction, however, that the bulk of the original untaxed imports was sold to the Indians, who, under Colonial law, were not supposed to indulge in alcoholic excitation.

The Coast Guard suffered a severe handicap against such tradition; they also lacked the intimate knowledge of local waters. Capture was the exception; escape was common. Time and again during pursuit the contact boats skittered away in the darkness, into some remote channel; following them meant grounding the government craft or collision with hidden rocks and reefs that would sink her. When pursuit was extremely hot, of course, the contact boat crews lightened cargo, and if necessary pitched every case overboard. But that did not mean that the stuff was irretrievably lost.

Cargoes went over the side with strong Manila lines connecting and supporting the cases; the lines led to semi-submerged buoys. With daylight, the crews were back, and while a lookout was kept to make sure of the non-reappearance of the Coast Guard, the loads were hauled and taken ashore in the regular manner. Another method was to use a flashlight in a five-gallon, weighted, carefully stoppered glass jug. This, when maintained a foot or so below the surface by a simple rock anchor, cast a dim submarine light, enough for the crews to return the same night and haul cargo and go.

When time pressed even more and the Coast Guard tracer fire was splattering around the boat, the cases were jettisoned as fast as possible, without the attachment of any lines or buoys. Bearings were taken on shore side landmarks, however, and depths and channel positions memorized. A clamming rake, a pair of long oyster tongs or eel spears could locate most of the cases the next day. But there was still a large element of loss in such situations, due to the action of local citizens. The noise, the display of tracer fire attracted them and they gave up sleep for the night, went forth as skirmishers to salvage what they could from rowboats, skiffs, canoes, motor launches. The drinking habits of an entire generation along the Eastern Seaboard were formed upon the consumption of free imported liquor. Golden Wedding drunk from a dripping-wet bottle was a favorite, and Dewar's mixed with a little sand, also Bacardi Gold Label and Martell Three Star brandy.

The Rum Row ship-to-shore service was forced into further effort to assure efficient delivery. Too much was being lost, either to the Coast Guard or the people who would not respect a smuggler's rights to reclaim what he had jettisoned. The contact boat crews, sailing out of Atlantic City went on strike, and one of them confided in a New York Times reporter. The rum-runner said that what they wanted was two dollars a case for the liquor they handled instead of one dollar, the current rate. The *Times* reporter quoted him as follows:

> "We go out and get the stuff and start back. We're fired on, and if we're close pressed, very often the cases go overboard. If we come back empty-handed, we get no pay at all. It's worth a dollar more a case, and we'll get it or no stuff comes in."

The handlers got their increase, and ingenuity, daring and guile were used in the transportation. Boats were built with double hulls which afforded compartment spaces that could be opened underwater in order to withdraw the liquor therein. The American fishing schooner *Marianne*, long suspected by the Coast Guard as a rum-runner, was finally seized on April 11, 1930, at New London,

Connecticut, and upon inspection was found to have a concealed hatch. This was under a cement-sealed wooden floor. The hatch gave onto capacious stowage room between the false keelson and the floor above, extended from the engine space aft all the way forward to the bow. The officers of the Coast Guard Section Base Four were so impressed that they had a naval architect's drawing made of the hull design. They also wondered how many thousands of cases had been carried into port aboard other supposedly legal vessels, the contraband underneath fish and ice and stout planking.

But daring was given forthright play in the Port of New York. The steamer *Hollywood* was loaded at St. Pierre with liquor worth half a million dollars. Then she was run down the coast close to New York. There she was camouflaged to resemble the *Texas Ranger*, a coastal steamer that was often in the port and well known to the Coast Guard. She came into the harbor in full daylight, moved on up through the Narrows and was reported as the *Ranger* at the Barge Office. A Coast Guard officer happened to be reading a shipping-news bulletin at the time, however, and he gleaned from it that the *Ranger*—what must be the real *Ranger*—was in the Gulf of Mexico.

A large hue and cry was begun. Some of its reverberations must have reached the bogus *Ranger*, for she fled at maximum speed for the protection of the upper Hudson River. She was abandoned, cargo and all, and her crew took to a ship's boat. They rowed desperately for Haverstraw, but it proved to be an inhospitable shore; the town police had been turned out, were waiting, and astern were Coast Guardsmen in impressive numbers. The seizure was the greatest to be made during Prohibition.

A similar attempt to put a bulk cargo ashore was undertaken at Montauk Point. The British-owned vessel *Audrey B.*, a 125-foot auxiliary schooner, made a bold sortie to satisfy the yuletide trade and was captured on Christmas Day, 1930, after a brief but dramatic chase. The night before, at three thirty in the morning, while patrolling in Block Island Sound, the Coast Guard boat *CG 290*, under the command of Chief Boatswain Alexander C. Cornell, had sighted the *Audrey B.* She looked like most any coastal fisherman, and after he had turned his searchlight upon her, Cornell did not think she was suspect. The holiday spirit prevailed aboard the *CG 290*; men shouted Christmas greetings over to the schooner. But she swung from her course and ran, and at once Cornell pursued.

Word had been passed from the Coast Guard base at New London that a mass delivery was planned by French and Spanish rum -runners working in conjunction with American bootleggers, and Cornell was determined to halt the schooner. His craft could produce a top speed of twenty-six knots, and he told the machinist's mate on watch that he wanted all of that. He had aboard as armament, in addition to the one-pounder cannon mounted on the fore deck, a Lewis gun, two .306 Springfield rifles and two Colt .45 automatic pistols. It was his conviction that he could do fairly well if the schooner crew proved to be recalcitrant.

Audrey B. changed course twice more in the thinning night, then ran straight for Fort Pond Bay, to the north and west of Montauk Point. She stood close past Montauk East Jetty Light, hooked around the West Jetty Light and Culloden Point, and entered the wide bay. Cornell took a look through his binoculars at the shore. Trucks were lined up on the dock, the New York convoy cars with them, and a crowd of men, ready to make the transfer from the schooner.

He told the *Audrey B.* to halt. The Coast Guard ensign was clearly visible at the masthead with the searchlight beam across it. Cornell did not delay any longer; he called the order to the one-pounder gunner. The range wasn't much and the gunner was expert. He fired three times and each shell went aboard the schooner. Her stem works disintegrated into a pile of shattered timber and her crew howled that they would surrender. She stopped as, on the dock, men waved their arms and cried out in blasphemy at the Coast Guard.

Cornell put his boat alongside her, made fast and boarded. She carried a crew of ten men. They gave no resistance when they were manacled and confined. Then Cornell took her in tow and started for New York. Her cargo, entirely contraband, was turned over to Customs. It consisted of twenty-eight hundred burlap sacks filled with straw-wrapped whiskey, and the estimate of its worth was calculated at one hundred thousand dollars, according to holiday-market prices.

Lamentation was loud in New York after the news of the seizure was published. But the most famous capture during Prohibition was that of the *I'm Alone*. It created a great amount of unfavorable publicity for the Coast Guard and was the cause of considerable international tension. The *I'm Alone* was a fast motor schooner under Canadian registry. Captain John T. Randell had sailed her for five years as a rum-runner, and, among seamen who knew him, was given about the same respect accorded Bill McCoy.

He cleared from Belize, British Honduras, on March 12, 1929, with a cargo of twenty-eight hundred cases of liquor. Hamilton, Bermuda, was his declared port of call. Nine days later and five hundred miles off his supposed course he was raised by the Coast Guard cutter *Wolcott* near Trinity Shoals on the Louisiana coast. He was outside the three-mile territorial limit but well within an hour's steaming distance of shore. The *Wolcott* ordered him to halt; he refused; a three-pound cannon shell was fired over his bow. But the schooner was too spry for the cutter and Randell hauled her away to sea.

The next day, he was picked up again by the Coast Guard, this time by the cutter *Dexter*. The *Dexter* had been in radio communication with the *Wolcott* and instantly gave chase. Randell had put the schooner two hundred miles from the American coast and he saw no reason why he should surrender to the Coast Guard. He held to his course, was fired upon as a consequence.

The cutter's gunfire was accurate. She sank the *I'm Alone*, although, marvelously, none of the schooner's crew was injured by her fire. When Captain Randell gave the abandon-ship order, however, a young French sailor was drowned before rescue was possible, and that gave strength to Randell's claim that the freedom of the seas had been violated.

The case generated vast coverage in both the American and the Canadian press. It became the contention of the Canadian government that the Coast Guard possessed no right whatsoever to fire upon one of her vessels two hundred miles from the coast. The American answer was the right of "hot pursuit," going back to the days of the War of 1812 and before. Precedents were cited and the "hot pursuit" validated by the fact that radio contact had been maintained between the two pursuing vessels. The Canadian government did not think much of that and national pride was inflamed, but finally subsided into arbitration. The non-Dry segment of the American population persisted in the theory that all Coast Guard operations which were concerned with rum running should be permanently suspended, and the Coast Guard reputation bore a blemish.

There were no other incidents involving seizures as great as those on the fake *Texas Ranger* and the *I'm Alone*. But there were many chases up and down the East River which the residents of Sutton Place could watch from the windows of their homes, and the inmates of Blackwell's Island could applaud, as New York City Police boats joined Coast Guard harbor craft. The rum-runners threaded the tidal rips of Hell Gate at top speed, ducked between tugs and tows, oil barges, rubberneck steamers, deep-sea ships putting in to Red Hook docks and U.S. Navy craft bound out from the Brooklyn Navy Yard.

Brief, sometimes bloody but usually unrecorded skirmishes were fought off lower Manhattan, in Buttermilk Channel, near the ramparts of Castle William on Governors Island and in the bay area between that and Staten Island. Commuters on the Manhattan-Staten Island ferries had their morning crossings enlivened by a good deal of marine hide-and-go-seek. The Jersey Central Railroad ferry patrons shared in the same sort of drama, and the residents of the Riverside Drive apartment houses often, at night, had their sleep punctuated by gunfire, looked out upon the Hudson to see the pursued scurrying nimbly from the law.

The citizens of the coastal towns had a greater number of alarms, excursions by night, chases and gunfights that gained prominence in the local news and are remembered vividly to this day. Staid, charming East Hampton, one of the loveliest villages on the Eastern Seaboard, had a real Christmas celebration after the events of December 21, 1922. A full gale thrashed the coast and brought ashore the schooner *Madonna V.*, just east of the Napeague Coast Guard station. She was small, thirty years old and began to break up fast, but her crew of eight men got off her safely.

They were made comfortable by the Coast Guard, although detained for an interview. The captain of the *Madonna V.* said that she was of Halifax, Nova Scotia, registry and that she was bound for St. Pierre from the Bahamas. The story smelled of rum running to the chief boatswain's mate in command of the station, and his suspicions were confirmed by what the East Hampton citizenry found upon the beach. Her cargo was choice assorted liquors. The *East*

Hampton Star described the salvage scene in its next issue; "willing hands" were used. Mrs. Jeannette Rattray, in her book of Eastern Long Island reminiscences, *Ship Ashore!*, gives further color:

"Lifelong teetotalers and even deacons of the church risked pneumonia in the December surf to bring it [cargo] ashore, prompted no doubt by the inherited custom of "wrecking" and old New England principles against waste of any kind... Wreckage from the schooner was strewn along the beach for miles to the westward."

The name of the *Madonna V.* was cherished in the township, and not for religious reasons.

East Hampton had other dubiously regarded visitors the next year. Mrs. Rattray, in the same book, tells of them with wry humor:

"The *Northcliffe*, a three-masted schooner, perhaps another "rum-runner" although that was surmise and she left no trail of evidence like the *Madonna V.*, went on the bar west of Georgica Coast Guard Station on May 18, 1923. She was from Nova Scotia; a vessel of some three hundred tons. Her captain, William McClouch, said he had lost his reckoning during a fog and southwest gale, and that they were bound from Turks' Island in the West Indies to Buckport, Maine, with a cargo of four hundred tons of salt. Local men who remember her well (Rattray's book was written in 1955) said the *Northcliffe* had been seen cruising off the Wainscott beach for a day or two. They think she was purposely run ashore, and that she hadn't a thing in her except a little whiskey. No salt. A Wainscott man saw her sails close in, the day she came ashore, when the fog lifted a bit. He called to a neighbor and they ran down to the beach. The seven men from the schooner were already ashore, bag and baggage, huddled up in the lee of the beach banks. The Captain asked to be directed to the nearest telephone."

The same year and the same month, two East Hampton High School girls came upon an abandoned oar dory while taking an early morning walk along Egypt Beach. It was pulled well up on the strand and was stowed to the gunwales with Scotch whiskey. The girls recognized the value of their find and the brand, and agreed to split the load equally between them. A volunteer squad was organized and the liquor safely stored. Then the girls went on to school, after duly notifying the Coast Guard at the Georgica Station and leaving a half a bottle, as they later told the story, "as a souvenir."

East Hampton's elm-lined Main Street often rumbled at night when thousands of cases of liquor from the Montauk Point beach-rendezvous landings were transported through it in truck columns towards New York. Residents became accustomed to the sound; only sleepless dogs barked and nobody except children asked questions. But the calm of Easter dawn, 1924, was rent when a six-cylinder Packard touring car turned into Woods Lane. It had the side curtains drawn, came from the direction of Montauk and was driven at fully sixty miles an hour. When it vroomed from Main Street into Woods Lane, six shots were fired at it by pursuers, a no-longer-patient group of Revenue agents.

It did not stop. Packard and pursuing government car kept on through the mists and primness of Bridgehampton, through Water Mill and into Southampton. There in the beach sand the Packard bogged, stalled, and the driver was apprehended. He admitted to being Pete Wells of Good Ground, and this was his second Prohibition offense. The Packard was freighted to the top struts with champagne.

Better luck rested with the majority of the men who violated the law, however, and many were aided by the popular dislike of enforcement. An outstanding example of Long Island sentiment was reported in the *East Hampton Star* in its issue of December 2, 1932. This was almost the end of Prohibition, but still the feeling existed as strongly as it had throughout the past decade. *The Star* said:

> "Mystery shrouds the identity of the boat which blew up last Saturday in Lake Montauk, and although it is reported that the boat had three fine Liberty motors and that all hands escaped, no one appears to know anything about the boat. At least if they do, they are not telling what they know."

The craft had just taken five hundred gallons of gasoline aboard at the dock. Then she moved out into the lake and started the run to the sea. But directly abeam the Montauk Yacht Club, very probably because of ignited gasoline fumes, she exploded into flame. One man of her crew was badly burned before he and his mates could abandon ship. The boat sank while they swam ashore in the sight of hundreds of spectators.

The Star account concludes: "While the boat was unquestionably a rum-runner or smuggler no information has been forthcoming as to its name or ownership."

An equal lack of interest in identifying the crew, coupled with widespread enthusiasm on the part of the villagers for her cargo, attended the arrival of the fifty-foot *Winifred H.*, an ex-fisherman, on the Napeague Beach on November 14, 1930. She held a potential endowment of eleven hundred cases and burlap sacks of whiskey, although the Coast Guard was on hand to confiscate most of it. Burghers and their wives and families waded waist-deep into the surf to retrieve bottles before the vessel lay high and dry with low tide. Coast Guard investigation showed that the craft had been stolen from her Sayville, Long Island, owner by rum-runners.

Bad luck also rode with the crew of the fifty-foot trawler *Sylvester*, which, with five hundred sacks of rye whiskey on her decks, was caught by the Coast Guard and surrendered off the surf line south of Montauk Point early in July, 1932. The *CG 937* cast a searchlight beam over her; when the Coast Guardsmen boarded, they found that she was fitted out as a swordfisherman. She carried plenty of expensive tackle, but no fish. Her crew gave their names as Ed Manes, Henry King and John Weltivet, all of Greenport, and the boat was towed to New York, where the men were held on Federal charges.

But there was real tragedy implicit in the abandonment of the contact boat *Francis*, which was grounded after sustained, concerted pursuit on Cedar Beach, between Sag Harbor and Shelter Island. She was a fast craft with three Liberty motors and was well known to the Coast Guard as a rum-runner. She was in a full cargo of whiskey when, in late November of 1932, she was picked up inward bound. Her speed allowed her to pull away from the first picket boat she met, but more were summoned by radio. They trapped her within a crisscross of searchlight beams and Lewis gun tracer fire as she spurted up the Shelter Island channel for the wooded reaches of Mashomack Point.

One of her three-man crew was believed by the Coast Guard to be her owner, and he was at the wheel. He grounded her rather than have her seized. Orders to halt were called again through the night. The search light beams fell fair upon the trio as, one by one, they jumped over the side into the shallows, splashed up onto the beach. Bullets struck closer in enfilade. A dark figure stumbled, dropped within the cerise mesh of fire. His mates helped him up and they ran on, supporting him, and were lost among the locust scrub past the beach.

The Coast Guard came ashore to inspect the boat and prepare to haul her off as a prize. They found on the trampled sand where the man had fallen a bloodstained lumberjack coat. It showed bullet punctures; without doubt the wearer had been severely wounded. Telephone inquiries were made at the Eastern Long Island Hospital at Greenport, the hospitals at Southampton and Riverhead. But no man bearing signs of gunshot wounds had been admitted to any of them. Doctors throughout the Eastern Long Island area were also questioned, said they had no record of such a patient. Whatever his hurt, the rum-runner was treated in privacy, either died or survived that way.

Stories that are now almost folk legend, but which in the main are verifiable, are told by old residents of the region. After another brush with the Coast Guard, a wounded rum-runner was carried for miles by his mates from the scene of the fight and the grounding of their boat in shallows off the south shore of Shelter Island. They were seen at dawn, offered aid and refused it. The wounded man was in mortal pain, however; a bullet had struck him in the stomach. His head lolled, his face was gray with death pallor and, though he suffered greatly, he made no sound.

A Greenport resident, the sole survivor of a family that once had engaged actively in rum running, made no particular secret of the fashion in which his father and brother died. The family owned a swift contact boat, went out one afternoon during the latter years of Prohibition to the Row for a load. While bound back towards Greenport, the boat caught fire from an overheated exhaust pipe.

All three men knew that in an instant she would explode fierily.

They chopped a hole through her bottom with a hatchet, in order to douse the fire and also in the hope that they might return and salvage her cargo. Then, wearing life jackets, they jumped over the side as she filled and sank.

The boat's position was off the area known as The Ruins, a marked reef at the northern end of Gardiner's Island. The tide was on the rise, would in time bring them across Gardiner's Bay to Orient Point or Plum Island. The survivor, an experienced fisherman, cautioned his father and brother not to overexert themselves, use their strength only to keep their heads out of water.

But there were contradictory, forceful currents between them and the land two miles away, and it was night, and the water was cold. The survivor heard the increasingly labored breathing of his father. He turned back to swim beside him, but it was already too late to save him. His father was face down, had just drowned, the thrust of the life jacket too great for the tired neck to support.

The survivor dog-paddled over towards his brother. He told him to hold on to his courage and persevere. He could make out Plum Island Light right ahead, recognized it, despite his exhaustion, by the characteristics of the beacon, white-flashing every seven and a half seconds. His brother was in trouble, yet he said that he could keep going a while longer. They drifted and dog-paddled slowly towards the light, the survivor occasionally holding his brother by the hand.

Then they were close beneath the tall white shaft of the lighthouse. The survivor gathered all his remaining strength and shouted for help. He shouted again and again, and the effort spent him. He was adrift from his brother, almost comatose when at last the lighthouse keeper heard him, came out onto the platform and lowered away the whaleboat in her davits.

He picked up the survivor, brought him into the lighthouse quarters, chafed him and warmed him. The survivor struggled hard to speak; he wanted to tell about his brother in the water. But it was more than half an hour before he could make the keeper understand. The keeper went out, then returned grim-faced; he had discovered the man's brother, but in the last half hour he had drowned.

The survivor, once back in Greenport, retired from the smuggling trade and became an oysterman. His skill was such that he was hired by the oyster companies to protect their beds against piracy, a rather common source of local livelihood. But the town still gained a vast share of its income from rum running. Some of the better-informed citizens who frequented Preston's Dock were greatly delighted one warm Sunday afternoon in summer by a scene that only they could appreciate.

A strapping chief warrant boatswain of the Coast Guard, who for several years had patrolled industriously in Long Island waters, was the source of the amusement. He had weekend liberty in port and a wife with social ambitions. After much persuasion, he agreed to sail with her aboard an ornate yawl owned by one of her new acquaintances and spend the day off Plum Gut.

Although the boatswain met a number of men aboard who were wearing rubber-soled shoes and yachting caps, it soon became his duty to sail the boat singlehanded. This he did, but with remarks to his wife which were not lost to the crowd on Preston's Dock. Towards sundown, sails stowed and under power, he headed in to berth the boat. Carouse dominated the cabin; the boatswain was alone in the cockpit.

He was about to draw alongside Preston's Dock when he was hailed from astern. The voice was familiar; it belonged to his father-in-law, a local man who was pre-eminent as a rum-runner. His father-in-law was just in from Rum Row. He stood at the wheel of his dark, low-hulled, fast launch, whiskey cases stacked about him. His gesture of greeting was full of friendliness. Then, when his son-in-law pretended not to see him, he called, "Hiya, George?"

The boatswain took a hand from the yawl's wheel. He shook it at his father-in-law. "Where," he asked, "are you going, you sonofabitch?"

His father-in-law was unperturbed. "Preston's," he said. "Give me room. The trucks are about due in from New York."

The boatswain told his father-in-law that if he followed the yawl into the berth, he, the boatswain, would forget all filial ties and break the man's neck. With further oratory that convulsed the dock crowd, he advised the rum-runner to get to hell and gone out of Greenport and stay gone. Then, his father-in-law convinced, the boatswain put the yawl alongside and secured her. But in the morning he sought out his commanding officer. He had asked for a transfer, it was learned along the grapevine that led from local Coast Guard headquarters. He was given it, detached and sent to Boston. Upon leaving, his father-in-law offered him a cheery farewell.

Famous once during Colonial rule when smugglers had used Sterling Cove as a haven, prominent in the eighteenth and early nineteenth centuries in the whaling trade along with adjacent Sag Harbor, Greenport had lived through good days created by the oyster business, slid into a decline that was halted by the increase of interest in yachting, built up fine local yards and then was given wealth by the rum running traffic. The town was ideally situated as a depot where rum-runners and bootleggers could meet, with Shelter Island, indented with numerous coves and inlets, to the south; the narrow extension of Orient Point to the east; Long Island Sound directly north of that; and out beyond to the southeastward, past Gardiner's Bay, the open Atlantic and Rum Row.

Greenport in the 1920's was a town of indiscriminate architecture where, upon two streets, the stores, a movie theater, a restaurant or so, a few garages, a pair of bowling alleys, a sailmaker and a chandlery served the residents and the neighboring fishermen, farmers and summer folks. The bootleggers, in collusion with the rum-runners, took it over after dark. The town police did very little to hinder the illegal operations, and there was very little that they could do.

Most of the town's population of less than ten thousand derived some form of profit from their disregard of the Prohibition law. Unemployment was practically nonexistent. Men strong enough to carry a case of liquor were hired and paid an average of twenty dollars a night to transfer the loads from the contact boats to the waiting trucks. The boatyards were busy at work on craft for which no contracts had been drawn but none were needed; everything the rum-runners ordered done was on a cash-in-advance basis. Gasoline was sold in five-hundred-gallon quantities. The town banks kept on hand large-denomination bills—one hundreds, five hundreds, thousands—for the deals out on Rum Row, and opened accounts for citizens who had never before in their lives owned more than a pair of seaboots and a clamming rake.

The trucks came in from New York with the approach of darkness. They were accompanied by the cars that would form the escort on the return, usually gray Buick touring cars. The Buicks, when the contact boats were in, took their own freight underneath the seats or concealed in false bottoms. While the bootleggers waited for the boats to appear from seaward, a group of four or five men attended to each car. They hefted it up and introduced between the chassis and the leaf springs a set of powerful coil springs about the size of a pound coffee can. These supported the extra weight of the loads; down the road to New York, if suspicious police or Revenue agents ranged close, there would be no telltale sag to inform them.

A good hour prior to the arrival of the contact boats, the bootleggers occupied the shore end of Main Street and the docks beside it. Nobody but their own people and others in their hire could enter the area. Hoodlums with pistols in their hands stood guard. A fisherman wanting to return aboard his own boat, customers seeking to cross on the Shelter Island ferry, were told to stay away until after dawn. If anyone insisted, he was clubbed over the head, kicked, hustled out of sight and kept very much incommunicado until past dawn.

The trucks formed in carefully aligned columns as soon as they were loaded for the more than one-hundred-mile run to New York. The scout cars moved ahead with a bevy of hoodlums in each, Thompson guns across their knees, pistols loose in the shoulder holsters, flashlights handy to signal back to the truck drivers or examine side roads for a possible hijacker ambush, pursuit by Revenue or state agents, and rarely, town police. Vannie Higgins, black-visaged, soft-spoken and murderous, was the bootleggers' anathema, and his specialty was the hijack operation, his zone of attack all of Long Island. The hoodlums watched squint-eyed for him and his co-workers. Behind them, alongside the column, were heavily armed outriders in other Buicks, and more of them maintained the rear guard.

The road they followed was winding and badly paved Route 25, which stretched at first through the flat potato farmlands and the little villages, then the brick buildings along Riverhead's Main Street and on out of Suffolk County into more populous areas. This stretch offered easy concealment to Higgins and in it he designed most of his roadblocks. Two cars would suddenly converge from a dark side road onto 25 and jam wheel to wheel; or a truck would be sent hurtling against the lead scout car. Then, from the roadside ditches, from behind trees, sometimes the corner of a crossroad gasoline station, the fire came.

It was not delivered in warning. It was meant to kill. Higgins was a man without mercy. His hijackers were partial to the submachine gun; they raked the convoys with intensive fusillades which the guardian hoodlums could not, in most instances, hope to match. But a furious exchange of shots lasted for a few minutes. The Higgins detachment usually moved in, tossing point-blank fire into the cars and truck cabs. The guards dead, wounded or in retreat, the truck drivers aware that in order to be paid they must remain alive, the cargo became Higgins's property.

Higgins's drivers mounted the trucks, took over the abandoned Buicks that were still worth driving. The dead and the wounded were removed from the highway, left for the attention of the police. Vehicles that blocked the road were shunted off it, and, under the new management, the convoys continued to New York. More than once, however, Higgins was beaten at his own game, out-shot and outmaneuvered, his hijackers trapped by sagacious bootleggers who had sent scouts in advance over the side roads along the prospective route. Other bootleggers relinquished the convoy system as unwieldy, chose to run the road in the faster, more operable Buicks or similar cars, or gladly paid the fee that allowed them the use of the Vanderbilt Speedway straight on into New York, with no hijackers, no police to menace them.

Back in Greenport, the night's work done, the bootleg labor force relaxed. Jo-Jo's, a speakeasy at the corner of Front and Main, so popular that it was established on the ground floor, received a lot of the custom. Fried clams, local oysters and French fries, needle beer and variously adulterated Rum Row brands were served. But the labor force paid for and got authentic whiskey. They could afford it, and many of them realized that never again would they have things so good.

Greenport first became active in the rum running trade on March 16, 1923, when an enterprising native landed 350 cases at Orient Point Wharf, a couple of miles beyond the village. Then, in April of the same year, the Coast Guard investigated what went on aboard a mysteriously navigated yacht, the *Magdalene*. She was a former U.S. Navy subchaser, owned by Mrs. Marie Magdalene Johnson, the wife of Dr. June Johnson of North Haven, Connecticut. The Coast Guard suspected the vessel of participation in liquor smuggling and she had been sighted often in Block Island Sound and further at sea, was frequently in Greenport waters. However, no actual proof could be discovered, despite the fact that one night in port the crew joined in a fight which very probably had to do with something other than ordinary wages and was severe enough to put the engineer, badly beaten, in the Eastern Long Island Hospital.

Federal agents outshone the Coast Guard on June eighth, when they were on hand at the Orient Point Wharf to greet the forty-foot contact boat *Charlotte*. She had aboard a cargo of Mountain Dew, an excellent Scotch that would have brought a premium price in New York. But a farm truck was commandeered by the agents and the Mountain Dew transferred onto it, along with the crestfallen members of the *Charlotte*'s crew. They vented their discomfiture on the ride to Greenport by pushing a very great part of the load off the truck. Nimble natives, among whom the smugglers had friends, gathered it up quickly; there was only token evidence left upon arrival, and the Charlotte crew did not bother to argue the charges brought against them.

Two weeks later, Vannie Higgins's hijackers struck between Greenport and Southold and seized a whiskey-laden truck on Route 25. There was a sharp gun fight, in which the armed guards escorting the truck were defeated. When police reached the scene, sixty cases were left. The rest, the vanquished said, a total of three hundred cases, had been seized, was now well on the way to New York.

The lack of police vigilance, the alarming deterioration of traditional calm along the main highway, brought about on July thirteenth the creation of the North Fork Law Enforcement Society. It was organized by representative citizens of Cutchogue, Orient, New Suffolk and East Marion. Their hope was to decrease, if not completely stop, hijacker depredations, rid Route 25 of the nightly bootlegger traffic, clean the rum-runners out of the Suffolk County harbors. It was ill-founded; the bootlegging trade continued very much as before.

But on September twenty-eighth a nameless fifty foot yacht and a Reo Speed Wagon onto which her one hundred cases of Rum Row liquor were being loaded were captured by Federal agents at New Suffolk. Then, on October nineteenth, the sloop *Clarence*, with five hundred cases aboard, fell into Federal grasp, and the schooner *Three Links* with six hundred cases. Christmas took on a bleak aspect for the absentee owners of twenty-six cases of rye found in a bungalow December twenty-first at Sandy Beach.

The Federals, keeping in fair stride, dug out at the Santford Brick Yard in Greenport on April 11, 1924, a collection of twenty cases of Scotch that had not yet been treated in the kiln. Inspirited, the Coast Guard came forward with a land seizure. They intercepted, on the way into Greenport from Orient Point, a prime haul of 560 cases, valued at twenty-eight thousand dollars and greatly grieved by the patrons of Jo-Jo's speakeasy.

Rum-runner losses mounted as spring and fair weather augmented the runs to the Row. The auxiliary sloop *Hattie* was caught, and the fine, high-powered speedboats *Pal* and *Nora*, and a whacking big load, one thousand cases, was seized in Mattituck Inlet. On August eighth, right in Greenport harbor, the big rum-runner *Pacific* was picked up with 659 cases aboard, her crew rueful but resigned.

Commander L. C. Farwell, in charge of the Coast Guard base at Greenport and working from his mother ship, the *Wyanda*, kept his fleet of boats on unremitting patrol, and also sent out landing parties. On the night of December nineteenth, one of these took as prize a truck loaded with Christmas cheer, bound for New York along Route 25, and headed her back into custody.

The sloop *Hattie T.*, a past transgressor, was captured again on the same date, along with the speedboat *Charles W. Simes*. This was off Montauk in chill, rough weather, but the two craft carried one hundred cases apiece. The sloop *Louise*, also trying for the Christmas market, made the run for shore and fouled with the Coast Guard; she had two thousand cases stowed high aboard her.

Commander Farwell was pleased with his men's record; on April 10, 1925, they towed into Greenport the speedboat *Sea Gull*, her cargo five hundred cases. Many contact boats were driven offshore before they could land and discharge, and Montauk became favored instead of Greenport as a rendezvous for the New York trucks. On the night of April seventeenth a detachment of hijackers, believed to be Vannie Higgins's men, went after an enormous quantity of liquor. It was worth $250,000 and was being moved in from Montauk. The hijack ambuscade was close to the Benson estate and, warned of its presence, Coast Guardsmen and State Police took their share in the ensuing gunfight. A State Police officer was wounded, and at Albany orders were given to tighten highway patrols.

Sensing the difficulties that lay ahead for them in the Montauk and Greenport areas, the really hard-bitten members of the contact boat fleet decided to shift further north. Their decision, of course, influenced the Coast Guard and, on September 1, 1925, the base at Greenport was given up, the *Wyanda* and the patrol boats transferred to Nantucket Island. Some of the Greenport smugglers saw this as a chance to renew contact with the Row. They put to sea in anticipation of the Christmas trade.

The Coast Guard base at New London extended its cordons, however, and on Christmas Day the fast boats *Pal*, *California* and *S. F. Burns* were caught. They were all running in big cargo, five hundred cases apiece, and the Coast Guard chivvied them, fired warning shots, made them slow and halt. The New London force kept keenly on duty; on June 29, 1926, the schooner *America*, with twelve hundred cases, was added to the record. On March 2, 1928, another mammoth haul was made in Mattituck Inlet, when fifteen hundred cases worth two hundred thousand dollars stayed a bit too long on the dock. On September 27, 1928, the schooner *Vinces*, with an estimated fifty-thousand-dollar load, ended her run off Greenport Harbor after firm orders to stop and surrender. But on January 2, 1931, the crew of the *Eleanor Joan* was less co-operative. They had aboard her one hundred thousand dollars' worth of liquor and they were determined to put it ashore in Greenport. Coast Guard gunfire was necessary to make them understand the meaning of the law.

Looking back over the Prohibition years, F. Langton Corwin, the editor and publisher of *The Suffolk Times* and a lifetime resident of Greenport, has a feeling of nostalgia touched with melancholy and a consciousness of the gravity of violating of the law. A quiet-spoken man, wearing the horn-rimmed glasses that have become a fixture for most of the practitioners of his profession, he has many stories to tell. He was empowered as a Notary Public during the rum-boom era. Nearly every day, he was approached by contact boat owners who wished him to witness the sale of their craft. These were, in the main, little more than titular transactions, done to avoid seizure and confuse the Federals and the Coast Guard. Mr. Corwin never accepted money for his services; he took instead a choice bottle of liqueur Scotch and was the envy of his neighbors.

He recalls the Coast Guard personnel he met—now all gone and part forgotten by the present generation—as a cross section of American society of that time. The first-enlistment men, the "boots" who came from circumstances of poverty in the South, were more likely than not to accept a bribe. They proposed to serve out one hitch, then return to their former life. Such abstract concepts as integrity, the good of the service, law and order, corruption and graft, were to them quite empty of import. But if a shipmate had been wounded in a sea fight, if one of Vannie Higgins's guerrilla squads had shot up the members of a landing party, the boots were implacable, even fierce in the execution of their duties.

As to the more experienced Coast Guardsmen, in particular the career chief petty officers, Mr. Corwin has an illuminating episode to relate. He was in a Greenport speakeasy one Prohibition evening, taking his leisure and enjoying a wee bit of contraband. A chief boatswain's mate sat at the table with him. Suddenly there appeared beside the chief's glass a thousand-dollar bill. Both the chief and Mr. Corwin regarded it in silence. No language was needed to emphasize the temptation. The chief commanded a patrol boat that maintained a segment of the Gardiner's Bay cordon. Tomorrow night, should he accept the bribe, he would run off course for an hour or so, keep his vision confined dead ahead while, astern, the contact boat with her Rum Row load passed inward to Greenport. The chief left the money on the table, and the next night, willfully, the rum-runner tried to slip past him and was captured.

But more dramatic than such tests of probity were the actions of the hoodlum guards in the hire of the New York bootleggers. Mr. Corwin and his wife had rented a summer cottage near a brickyard in the outskirts of Greenport, and had there as guests for an evening's cards Dr. and Mrs. Courtland Jennings of the village. The game lasted late and the Corwins offered to drive the other couple home in the family car. Corwin left through the brickyard gate that debouched upon Route 25.

A New York-bound liquor convoy was moving along the highway. Scout cars passed, full of tautly hunched hoodlums peering through the side curtains. Trucks followed, and then the outrider cars, and abruptly one of the latter drew close beside the Corwin machine. Corwin was forced to drive into the ditch. Two men leapt from the outrider car; they held Thompson guns and a flashlight. Mrs. Corwin screamed under the dazzling exposure of the flashlight beam. She was told roughly to shut her mouth. A hoodlum wanted to know, who the hell were they—Revenuers?

No, Corwin assured the interrogator. Neither he and his wife nor the doctor and his wife were in any way affiliated with the enforcement of the Volstead Act. He gave their names, explained the card game and the offer to drive the Jennings home.

Then he was asked, why, for Crissakes, was he coming out of a dark brickyard? Guys got shot like that.

Corwin explained that he had rented a cottage behind the yard, was in the habit of using the yard gate to and from Route 25.

The hoodlum and his companion considered the statement, conferred. So get going, Corwin was told. And make it fast.

Corwin did, just as fast as he could shift gears. But the hoodlums' car tagged his into Greenport and right to the Jennings's home on Main Street. Mrs. Corwin had conquered her temptation to hysteria, but still Corwin delayed their return to the cottage for two hours. It was safer, he knew; his wife was no more nervous than that pair of hoodlums, and they were armed with Thompson guns.

CHAPTER ELEVEN

As a logical consequence of the popular shoreside sentiment about the liquor problem, the Coast Guard found that a serious number of transgressors were among yachtsmen and sport fishermen. These held to the idea that to break the law, to aid and abet rum running, somehow created no serious harm. Often enough, a big power cruiser finished a weekend coastwise sail with a couple of cases of Rum Row whiskey under the floorboards in the motor compartment, or the crew of a sailing yacht artfully stuck their liquor, bottle by bottle, between old jibs, staysails and miscellaneous gear in the forepeak.

Sportsmen after tuna and swordfish off the Atlantic coast lent their presence aboard to the seemingly legitimate actions of charter-boat owners who were in reality professional rum-runners. Yachtsmen who derived both pleasure and good liquor from the arrangement let rum-runners fly club burgees as camouflage, even in some instances allowed the use of their boats for sorties to Rum Row.

Atlantic City, with a complex of canals and creeks around it, Long Beach, similarly situated, and Jones Inlet were all recognized rum-runner bases from which the smugglers put out for a load on each night of reasonably fair weather. Coast Guardsmen patrolling off them knew that many of the "party boats" were not such, that the "trial" and "test" runs made from a number of boatyards were concealed efforts to reach the Row. They were fired upon in the observance of their duty. Contact boats about to be caught often used rifle fire to douse the Coast Guard searchlights during night chase, smash the lenses, wound or, if necessary, kill those who directed the beams. Coast Guard craft closing in on a suspect had collided at full speed with whiskey cases deliberately jettisoned to sink or at least halt them, and they had been forced to limp into port with split bows and strakes, the pumps just about able to take the strain. For them there was no aura of charm about the men they pursued.

But on weekends, hundreds of solid citizens became the associates of criminals and delighted in flouting the law. A Coast Guard picket boat that pulled alongside a suspect craft could not fire. Mayors, judges, lawyers, doctors, businessmen were at the rail, exhibiting rods and the day's catch, threatening demotion or transfer to distant, isolated stations for the Coast Guard crew if the boat were stopped and searched.

The crew of the Coast Guard destroyer *Hiram Paulding* were given evidence once more of both the cunning and the ruthlessness of the rum-runners, while on duty off the port of New York on Washington's Birthday, 1925.

Lookouts aboard her raised four contact boats proceeding to seaward from the lee of Sandy Hook. Her captain, John S. Baylis, now Commodore, retired, was notified and came onto the bridge. He regarded the quartet and assumed that its purpose was rum running. The time was late afternoon, and the obvious ploy for the four boats was to break formation, avoid the destroyer and swing past her to the Row.

Baylis ordered the deck awnings stowed, the cover stripped from the forward three-inch cannon, told the engineer officer on watch to fire all four boilers; he wished the maximum speed of twenty-six knots. When the *Paulding* began to kick up a wide-curling wash with her increase of momentum, two of the rum-runners turned back, shaped courses for Sandy Hook and their very probable home port, Atlantic Highlands, inside it. Commodore Baylis told the radioman to communicate with the shore station at the Hook so that picket boats would be sent out to make an intercept.

But the other two contact boats were boiling merrily along for the Row. Commodore Baylis let his gunnery officer work out trajectory and range, then gave the fire order. A shell from the first bracket very nearly took the bow out of one of the contact boats.

All that could be seen of her from the bridge of the *Paulding* was spray and exhaust vapor. Then she hove to, and her partner along with her. Commodore Baylis said that he wanted to talk with their captains and they were brought to the destroyer's bridge.

They were young men, sea-browned, husky, dressed in neat if soaked khakis. Commodore Baylis asked, "Why did you stop?"

A pensive smile accompanied the answer. "Cap, if spray and shrapnel came aboard you like that, you'd stop, too."

But the Commodore was not satisfied, and only part of his plan had been put into execution. Gazing to seaward, he saw that the other pair of boats from the original quartet had not gone into Atlantic Highlands, but had only feinted in that direction. While he was making his capture of this pair, the others had scurried for the Row, loaded and started back. Baylis calculated distance, speed and the radius of the arc the *Paulding* could describe and still catch them. He ordered the bridge telegraph set at Flank Speed, and the big destroyer jumped with the propeller thrust.

The second pair ducked, dodged, put up a smoke screen and tried a number of desperate evasive tactics. But then they hove to, shells from the *Paulding* too close, and surrendered. Baylis sent crews from the destroyer aboard the captured boats. The Coast Guardsmen, armed, took them off towards the Row, and the hunt continued late into the night. Before dawn, seven contact boats were captured and hung up on lines astern of the destroyer. The Commodore enjoyed a good-night cup of coffee in the wardroom and turned in, weary. But he had left orders that the rum-runner crews, some twenty men in all, be kept in one of the boats astern. He did not want them aboard his vessel. A concerted rush on their part might injure, even overcome his crew.

Commodore Baylis was in the bunk and asleep when he was aroused by the sharply called bridge order, "Full astern!" Then he felt the vessel tremble as the engines were reversed, and while he ran for the bridge, he heard, "Man overboard!" It was one of the prisoners from the towed boat; he had been pitched into the sea.

Sailors from the *Paulding* hauled the spluttering man out, while his fellows sat in glum silence. Commodore Baylis questioned him on the bridge, and once the sea water was out of his lungs, the man talked. Some of the captured rum-runners were from Brooklyn, he said. The others were from New Jersey. But more than geography separated the two groups.

A contact boat hailing from New Jersey had recently been caught by a Coast Guard picket boat off Sandy Hook. Her crew had been stubborn; they had been fired upon before they surrendered and one of their number was wounded. The Coast Guardsmen were merciful. When the rum running boat was secured at the dock, they started to carry the wounded man across the lonely marshy wastes of the government reservation behind the Hook and to the nearest hospital.

It was night and very dark; mist was in over the marshes from the sea and the Coast Guardsmen were extremely tired. They were beset by hoodlums who worked in alliance with the rum-runners. The fight was short but severe and in it a Coast Guardsman was gravely hurt, flung face down into a quicksand stretch of swamp where he might very well have sunk and died. His companions saved him with great difficulty, and meanwhile the wounded smuggler was spirited away to freedom.

This fact was known to the Brooklyn rum-runners aboard the boat towed by the *Paulding*. They would face interrogation in New York in the morning, then trial, and because of the Sandy Hook incident things would go hard for the entire group. So one of the New Jersey men had been offered to the sea as sacrifice.

Such brutality kept the Coast Guard keen, eager to perform the Rum Row duty. Young officers just down from their four years at the academy in New London, and newly enlisted men, too, were reminded of the famous case of Jim O'Connell. The wariness which had brought about his capture in 1925 was constantly employed.

The *Hiram Paulding* had been cruising off Fire Island Inlet with the scallop fleet between her and the shore on a bonny summer day. She passed within a mile of the fleet and she was a splendid sight with her bow wash aglitter, her four lean stacks, the bright red-and-white-barred ensign and the foaming, flashing wake. Fishermen usually knocked off work for a moment when they saw her, gave a wave of the hand. Today, however, the two men seated on the deck of a big scalloper held their heads lowered, seemed very busy with their shucking knives.

The officer of the deck reported the circumstance to Commodore

Baylis when the destroyer had steamed on beyond the scallopers and to the eastward. "Those guys on the big boat didn't look up or wave, sir," The Commodore at once gave the order for the *Paulding* to double back on her course. A boat was swung out and a boarding party went over to the scalloper.

A compactly stowed cargo of seven hundred cases of Rum Row whiskey was in her hold. Her captain, one of the two exceptionally busy men seated on deck, was Jim O'Connell. He was notorious as a rum-runner captain, maintained high rank in the Big Bill Dwyer combine that operated with New York City as a base. On the bridge of the *Paulding*, he told Commodore Baylis, "I ain't got no argument. Three years now since I've been picked up."

But before he was through, Jim O'Connell talked about his boss. Big Bill Dwyer, handsome, wealthy, well educated, was also indicted eventually for his transgressions of the law and sent to serve two years in Atlanta. He was an almost heroic figure in the New York sporting world, one of the officials of the New York Hockey Club, an intimate of Jimmy Walker's gay night-life circle and a participant in many activities besides that of the illegal liquor combine he controlled. Frank Costello was reputed to have his thin, skillful hands in each of those activities, and to possess the brains that ran the combine.

Communication between the Federal penitentiary at Atlanta and New York was kept up while Big Bill served his sentence. A Coast Guard officer who knew Jim O'Connell was informed of this by chance. The rum-runner captain had lately been freed from his own legal entanglement and was in an ebullient mood when the officer met him on lower Broadway. The newspapers still carried profuse stories about "the King of the Bootleggers"; Dwyer was missed on his home heath. But, O'Connell said, he went regularly, once a week, to Atlanta. There he talked with Big Bill, who was living very well. Big Bill gave him his orders for the combine, and on his return to New York, O'Connell passed them on to Costello to be considered and then executed.

The Coast Guard officer parted pleasantly from O'Connell and sent the information he had gleaned to superiors in New London. It so happened that Mrs. Mabel Walker Willebrandt, the Assistant United States Attorney General in charge of all Prohibition prosecutions, was a guest at a New London dinner party right after the information was received. She was apprised of Big Bill's mode of life at Atlanta. The following week, there was a new warden at the Federal penitentiary and Big Bill was given enormous trouble handling his complex affairs for the rest of his prison term.

But even when he was released from the penitentiary, he learned that the smuggler's path was thorny. Vast sums were needed to conduct the trade, and, only strongly financed combines could operate at a profit. Rum Row was being driven farther and farther out to sea. The Supreme Court had rendered a decision regarding Prohibition on April 11, 1927. It was historic, and it stated under the title, "Ships Seized Not Immune from Prosecution, George Ford v. United States (Quadra), (273 U.S. 593)," that ships carrying illicit cargo should and would be seized upon the high seas. The case had to do with the seizure of a British-flag vessel off the California coast.

She was the *Quadra* and was picked up by the Coast Guard with a full cargo of liquor aboard, outside United States territorial waters. Then she was towed into San Francisco, where her captain and other officers were convicted of conspiracy to violate the National Prohibition Act and the Tariff Act of 1922. The court decided that the seizure was in accordance with the terms of the treaty of May 22, 1924, between the United States and Great Britain. "Adjudication of the vessel," in the ruling of the Supreme Court, upholding the original conviction, not only meant the loss of the vessel herself. It meant that anything aboard was liable to seizure and the responsible members of her crew were liable to prosecution.

Additional Supreme Court rulings which dealt hard blows to the Rum Row traffic were passed on May 31, 1927. One declared that a United States-flag vessel registered in the coastwise trade but carrying liquor thirty-four miles at sea could be legally seized. A second upheld a lower court's decision convicting a United States-flag vessel of conspiracy to violate the Prohibition and Tariff Acts, upon evidence obtained through the Coast Guard's search and seizure on the high seas beyond the twelve-mile limit.

Costello, pondering these things with Big Bill Dwyer and the others still willing to conspire, realized that the mother ships bearing the supply sources must roam far offshore. The problem created for the bootleg syndicates also affected the Coast Guard as the

messages from the clandestine radio stations went out to the syndicate vessels at sea, to stay at least ninety miles from the coast except
in extremely foul weather. The patrol work was tremendously
enlarged; Coast Guard ships followed the rum-runners in obdurate
day-and-night pursuit.

The usual tour of duty was five days at sea, five days of stand-
by in port while repairs were made, then five days of liberty. This
was for men on the seagoing destroyers that often cruised more
than one hundred miles from the coast, the cutters and the 125-foot
diesel patrol boats. An average complement aboard a destroyer or
cutter was one hundred men, and eighteen or nineteen for the 125-
footers. Most of the older men among the officers and petty officers
were married, and rarely was there a man without some sort of fem-
inine attraction waiting for him ashore. Liberty was treasured. But
when at sea, after a suspected rum-runner had been sighted,
thought of it had to be put aside. The orders were to keep in
pursuit until an arrest was possible, or fuel, stores, and water had
run dangerously short.

The *Monaghan* had been rolling up and down the shoulders of
waves along the Atlantic coast for weeks of monotonous patrol in
the summer of 1929 when her lookouts caught the white glimmer
of sails at the seaward horizon. The destroyer was ninety miles out
from Long Island and her captain was curious. He took the bridge,
examined the other vessel, a fine sailing yacht, in his glasses and
told the quartermaster to point up for her,

The gilt lettering on her counter and the neat legends on her life
rings proclaimed her to be the *Surf*. She was in excellent shape, her
white hull impeccable, her varnish freshly swabbed down, her cabin
skylight opened to the fresh easterly breeze which she sailed under
all canvas. The captain of the *Monaghan* not only admired her, he
felt a small twinge of envy. The man who appeared to be her owner
was seated at his ease in the cockpit, legs stretched and a long,
light-hued cigar clamped between his teeth. He wore a visored cap
that bore within gold-embroidered crossed anchors the emblem of
a famous Long Island yacht club. His wave of greeting to the
Monaghan was genial, but he kept the strapping big schooner right
on course for the coast, his sails balanced nicely to the wind thrust,
and when he called out for the steward, his voice held authority.

The steward came up the companionway ladder from the cabin with celerity. He wore a starched white jacket and held a silver salver on which was a tall Scotch and soda. The man at the wheel took the drink and sipped it; the captain of the *Monaghan* thought of the weekend he might be spending ashore and his envy increased. Still, there was for him something almost too perfect about this scene. It was a yacht brokers' dream, and more. Perhaps it was just very clever play-acting—and yet, out here, he decided that he had no right to halt, board and search the *Surf*. The captain ordered the *Monaghan* to keep parallel course to the west with the *Surf*; he would stay with her until she made port, or at least was within the twelve-mile limit.

Dusk darkened the sea as the two ships approached the coast, the last sunset light crimson on the schooner's topsails. Fire Island Light Ship was dead ahead. It was time, the captain of the *Monaghan* knew, that the schooner either changed course for the westward and New York or hauled around for Montauk Point; she was of too deep draft to enter Fire Island Inlet. She came about gracefully, crossed the wind and stood away for Montauk. But she was now within the twelve-mile limit and gradually, very gradually slipping in towards the Long Island shore.

The captain of the *Monaghan* took another look at the man in the schooner's cockpit. He had added a brass-buttoned blue flannel blazer to his costume with the dusk chill. The expensive buckskin deck shoes were still propped negligently on a side settee. A new cigar replaced the several that he had smoked. The steward reappeared with a fresh drink, his white jacket still very correct.

But the *Monaghan*'s captain sensed keenly that all this was part of make-believe for his delusion. He ordered a whaleboat swung out and sent a boarding party into it under the command of a young ensign. Before the boat was lowered and he called across to the schooner to heave to, he spoke a few quiet words to the ensign. Then, from the bridge wing, he watched alertly.

The schooner lay with her emptied sails softly buffeting the shrouds. The whaleboat reached her in a smooth run and the ensign boarded. His voice and that of the man in the blazer could be heard from the destroyer's bridge. The wearer of the blazer vigorously protested any search of the schooner. An injunction was needed, he said, and without one he would not permit it. His vessel had in no way broken the law.

The ensign agreed to that. He was very polite. But the Coast Guard, he pointed out, had the right to examine any vessel and check her registration numbers as demanded by law. Those were carved into the main beam in the cabin, said the man who wore the blazer. And the ensign could not go below. "The ladies are dressing for dinner."

"Tell them to turn their backs," the ensign said. Then he went below.

He hailed the captain of the *Monaghan* after he had finished his search. There were no ladies aboard the schooner, he said. Instead, all of the cabin space was occupied by cases of whiskey. His preliminary count brought the total to approximately four-thousand, Scotch and rye. The captain of the *Monaghan* told him to bring the sartorial smuggler and the steward accomplice aboard the destroyer as prisoners. A towline was reeved around the anchor windlass on the *Surf*, a Coast Guardsman took her wheel and the *Monaghan* started for New York. The ensign stood with his captain for a moment in the bridge wing, staring astern at the tow. "Maybe, sir," he said, "I'll never have the chance to refuse again. But the fancy fella who was aboard over there tried to slip me ten thousand dollars not to go below. He must've wanted me to think those women were strictly bare-tail."

There were very few rum-runners who were talented enough to produce the artistic flourishes given the Monaghan by the *Surf*. Most of the lot working at their trade between Block Island and Montauk Point in the last years of Prohibition were prone to fight rather than pretend. An excerpt from the official Coast Guard reports, dated February 17, 1930, shows this with some grim, simple detail. Boatswain Alexander C. Cornell, mentioned in the report as captain of the *CG 290*, had become the smugglers' scourage and engaged them implacably whenever possible. It was he who ended up the year with the Christmas Day capture of the *Audrey B.* taking from her twenty-eight hundred cases of assorted liquor. The report reads:

At 1610 left Base Four. (New London, Connecticut) At 1740 position Latimers Reef light. Sighted gas screw *Gander*

heading out. Hove her to at Napatree gas buoy and boarded her. No violations. Arthur Rowland, Master; crew five.
When released she stood out Watch Hill passage. Waited
until she was nearly obscured and commenced trailing her
at full speed on E and S course. Passed about two miles
North of Sandy Point and rounded Block Island at about
same distance. At 1945 passed Block Island Southeast light
abeam and heading SxE. At 2000 *Gander* laid to and spoke
to another speed boat, both dark. 2005 continued full speed
off shore on course SxE. At 2100 sighted signal light of contact vessel bearing SWx1/2 W. Patrol boat laid to until 2145.
Maintained sharp lookout. At 2145 proceeded SW, full speed
at 2150. Located *Black* ahead. 2202 put searchlight on her,
distance 100 feet. *Gander* alongside starboard side and leaving. Contact boat getting under way. *Gander* crossed ahead
of *Black* and *CG 290* passed close astern of *Black*. No name
visible. 3 blank one-pounder shells were fired. Name
Gander was seen on stern of speed boat. Sacks of liquor
were on deck and in dory. She made no effort to heave-to.
Four 1-pounder service shells and one pan of machine gun
ammunition were fired into her. One-pounder did not come
back to battery. Recoil spring was found to be broken and
firing of the one-pounder was discontinued. 2210 *Gander*
stopped and *CG 290* went slow to go alongside when she
threw out a smoke screen and went ahead turning right all
the time. The *CG 290* kept just clear of smoke screen and
fired two pans of machine-gun bullets into her, all shots
seeming to hit her. In the meantime the *Black* had got up to
windward of us and had also sent out a smoke screen making it impossible to see. As both these vessels were much
heavier than the patrol boat and believing they were making
an effort to ram us went full left to try and get clear of
smoke. Was unsuccessful, so turned full right and cleared.
Made careful search with glasses. Only one vessel could be
sighted. Ran her down and found her to be [*Black*] contact
boat. Then turned and searched vicinity but could not
relocate the *Gander*.

The report, after Cornell's statement, concludes:

Boatswain Cornell having found that the *Gander* had run away from him immediately sent a radio message to the Base reporting same. The *CG 135*, *CG 148* and *CG 234* which were at the Base were stationed in Fishers Island Sound, off the Dumpling [reef], and East of the Race. At about one o'clock of February 7th the motors of the *Gander* were heard to the Northward of Sandy Point. At about 0145 were heard off Watch Hill entrance by the *CG 212*, already on duty. Half an hour later the *CG 234* picked up the motors and upon using her searchlight located her wake and smoke screen and proceeded at full speed firing two one-pounder blanks. The *CG 135* lying in the Race, seeing the *Gander* and her smoke illuminated by the *CG 234* searchlight intercepted the *Gander* and fired into her seven pans [three hundred rounds] of machine-gun ammunition at various ranges and followed the *Gander* while so doing from the Race to the Bartlett Light Vessel. The *Gander* attempted to get into Niantic Bay but could not accomplish this and was subsequently followed to Saybrook. Off Saybrook Point she was fired at by the *CG 241*.

7 February. *CG 231* at Montauk; *CG 212* at Watch Hill; *CG 288* at Bridgeport searching; *CG 241* searching from Bridgeport to the Westward; *CG 284* searching New Haven to Bridgeport for *Gander*; *CG 290* searching from Saybrook to New Haven for the *Gander*; *CG 135* searched the Connecticut and Thames Rivers for the *Gander*.

Note: The *Gander* surrendered to the Collector of Customs at New London, at 1230, 11 February 1930.

The *Gander* and her sister vessel, the *Goose*, both fifty-nine-footers equipped with splendid, high-powered triple Liberty motors, had run long and successfully out of Greenport, then farther up the coast. When the well-riddled *Gander* was surrendered by her crew at New London, Boatswain Cornell was marked high on the smugglers' hate list, but even before that he had lost any chance of receiving their warm regard.

His boat, the redoubtable *CG 290*, had been a rum-runner in her day, under the name of *Black Duck*, and Cornell had engaged her in a bloody, zigzag night fight off Newport. That was in the year preceding his pursuit of the *Gander*, and he had been even more determined when he found her making an attempt to enter Newport Harbor. He was on patrol out of Base Four at New London, and the *Black Duck* was ghosting in from seaward, well laden with Rum Row cargo.

Cornell challenged her from the pilothouse of his patrol boat. He put his searchlight upon her and called to her to heave to. She gave him a great burst of speed as answer, and her crew, with a curved piece of thick boiler iron protecting them against fire from aft, must have thought themselves safe. She slashed a creamy wake and the Liberties roared wide, and then a smoke screen was flung out astern. Cornell pursued and fired. One bullet out of every six in his machine-gun ammunition was a tracer, and he could check his aim by their luminous flight.

He was squarely on target time and again, even heard the bullets rip into the rum-runner's transom, clang in ricochet from the boiler-plate shield. This summer night, the Atlantic fleet, on cruise, was at anchor in the harbor, and around the warships were many yachts and coastal vessels. The *Black Duck* laced a course through the fleet, her motors strident, her wake a vast, pale splatter that roiled out upon the calm harbor waters and made anchor cables surge and tighten. Cornell cut through her wake and added his own to the disturbance; at the boat boom of a Navy ship an outraged coxswain shouted before he jumped for his life. The combined wash of the rum-runner and the Coast Guard craft had banged his running boat hard against the warship's side, had sprung and sunk her.

Cornell held on in pursuit. He let his Lewis gun cool for a bit while the *Black Duck* looped for the harbor mouth and set off along the coast in the direction of Providence. Then, at close range, before his ammunition was exhausted, he fired pan after pan. The *Black Duck* evaded him when he could no longer fire, and he broke off the chase. But the next day, near Providence, the rum-runner was discovered on the beach.

All of her cargo was gone. She had been hurriedly swabbed down, although Coast Guard inspection revealed bloodstains. Three men of her crew had been killed by Cornell's fire, and the remainder were rounded up, arrested and tried in the Federal Court at Providence. The case was given enormous newspaper and radio coverage, and Cornell, knowing himself to be a marked man, could have asked for transfer from his Base Four duty. But he stayed, eager to continue his work against the men who threatened him.

With the *Black Duck* case in mind, the Coast Guard put on a rather stark display the day of the Yale-Harvard boat races in June of 1931. They had frequently issued warnings to yachtsmen regarding the misuse of club burgees by rum-runners. When the hundreds of yachts entered the Thames River at New London for the gala event, they passed the sleek, dark-hulled *Whispering Winds*, anchored in midstream. She was a big, powerful craft with a solidly built pilothouse, double motors and a sport-fishing pulpit out over the bow. She flew a white-starred jack on her bow staff and the burgee of a reputable yacht club at her masthead. The forward windows of her pilothouse had been punctured by Coast Guard gunfire, however, and on deck were stacked sacks of whiskey that bore, plainly enough for any yachtsman to read, the distiller's description of her cargo—Highland Still. She had been seized recently off Block Island after hot pursuit.

But, whatever the effect upon the yachting fraternity, the smugglers were not dismayed. They had already taken for granted the death of the captain of the Canadian schooner *Josephine K.* in early spring, 1931. The schooner had ventured inside the twelve-mile limit, run towards The Race when pursued and discharged her cargo into a garbage barge sent out under tow by a New York syndicate to make rendezvous with her. Orders to halt were ignored. Shots were fired and one killed her captain, William P. Cluett, while he stood at the wheel. Later, the Coast Guard picked up the barge. She carried aboard only part of the *Josephine K.*'s cargo, but it was estimated as being worth three hundred thousand dollars when brought in to New London. The men whom Cornell and his Base Four shipmates sought on patrol gambled their lives for consistently high stakes.

Cornell had the converted *Black Duck*, now the *CG 290*, on patrol the night of August 20, 1931, and sailed inside The Race. The wide sweep of the Cornfield Point Ship beacon was off his port bow several miles distant when he raised the lights of a Sound steamer to the eastward. The steamer's silhouette was easily recognizable; she made her nightly run here past the light vessel, proceeded on towards New York. But Cornell decided to stand in close alongside her; there was a slight, strange patch of shadow under her counter.

He closed, lying almost directly in the steamer's course, then doused his lights and rang for the motors to be stopped. The *CG 290* lay motionless, silent. The bluff old steamer thudded past, her deck lights casting a band of radiance onto the sea, her passengers sleepily waving from the rail; the mate on watch and the lookout were staring tensely aft.

Then a lightless rum-runner—she proved to be the *Artemis*—lunged out from under the steamer's counter. She had been captured by the Coast Guard three times previously, each time bought back, at great cost to her owners, at public government auction. Her crew were convinced that tonight she would escape. Motors turning at full revolution, she headed straight at the *CG 290* to ram.

Cornell moved very fast. He signaled his engine man to kick one of the double propellers ahead, the other astern. He spun the wheel to avoid being rammed bow-on and then grasped the Lewis gun. The *Artemis* hit his craft a glancing, but rending blow; he was too late to veer completely out of her course. But he poured the Lewis fire down into the rum-runner and he kept it going when she jounced on and slanted for shore.

He pursued her and drilled her length with more than five hundred rounds. She put up a smoke screen that blinded him; the man at her wheel sailed her with desperate skill; her motors still shoved her at maximum speed. He lost her along the intricacy of her zigzag courses, at last reluctantly gave up the chase.

When full speed was taken from the *CG 290* and the fore part of the vessel lowered back into the water, she leaked badly. The attempt to ram had torn an entire plank out of her bow structure. It was necessary to stuff the leak with mattresses from the crew's bunks to keep her afloat. With tender care Cornell headed her for Base Four to report.

The morning of August twenty-first, headquarters at New London got in touch with local and state authorities in both Connecticut and

New York. A search was made of all boatyards within a hundred-mile area; the usual rum-runner procedure after a smuggler had been fired upon by the Coast Guard was to haul the bullet-marked craft out onto the ways, replace the telltale planking with new. But there was no immediate discovery of the *Artemis*, although picket boats had also combed the Sound, and fishermen and yachtsmen had been questioned. Then a telephone call came in to New London and the Coast Guard headquarters staff was grateful.

The call was from the district attorney at Oyster Bay, on the North Shore of Long Island. He related a story that had bizarre elements. The night before, a yacht had been boarded while lying at the anchor in Cold Spring Harbor, near the town. The owner had been shot to death and his wife abducted during a scuffle with the pair of men who had boarded the ship. Due to the Coast Guard alarm about the *Artemis*, the Oyster Bay district attorney had been informed of gunfire heard on the Sound. He had believed that it might possibly be connected with the local murder and abduction. Another telephone call he had just completed had located two men suffering from gunshot wounds in the Eastern Long Island Hospital at Greenport. The men were under guard, but they did not appear to be the murder-and-abduction pair. It was much more likely, the Coast Guard told the district attorney, that they were members of the crew of the *Artemis*.

During the course of the conversation with Base Four and Oyster Bay, a Coast Guard seaplane had put down at New London. It carried a group of officials from Washington on a tour of inspection. Commodore Baylis, at that time chief of staff of the Destroyer Force at the base, asked permission to borrow the plane and its pilot. This was granted, and they flew southwestward, over Plum Island and Orient Point.

Circling high above Orient Point, they discerned what looked to them like a well-rehearsed movie mob scene. Hundreds of people were scrambling up through the crab grass and sand of the bluff about three miles west of the point. The people, when the plane dived low, were seen to be hefting whiskey cases or bottles in sacks. Skiffs still partially loaded with cases were inside the surf line on the beach. This, no doubt, was the cargo from the *Artemis*, which had been transferred to the skiffs along with the wounded men during the night, after she had eluded the *CG 290*.

A radio message was sent by Commodore Baylis to the nearest patrol boats. He ordered them to land men at the beach and seize the contraband. Then the plane took to the water and Commodore Baylis and the pilot went ashore. The mob scene was rapidly dissolving. Whiskey-burdened figures thrashed through the bushes at the crest of the bluff, jumped into cars and fled. But thirty cases had been left buried in the beach sand and, with the skiff loads, represented a sizable capture. The commodore sat down on an empty case in the sun to wait for the arrival of the patrol boats before he went to question the wounded men in the hospital at Greenport.

But the search for the *Artemis* continued, with the help of the authorities throughout the Sound area. She was found on the haulway of a boatyard in Port Jefferson, Long Island, some miles distant from the site where her cargo had been landed. The Coast Guard had no right to seize her once she was out of the water. However, there was new planking in her bow and transom, and the scrap heap at the yard was examined. It contained not only bullet-marked planks, but the plank that had been torn from the bow of the *CG 290* when the patrol craft was rammed.

A United States marshal was stationed at the yard in expectation of a visit by the owners of the *Artemis*. They arrived in time and eventually the boat was seized. The crew were arraigned in Federal Court, tried and convicted on charges impossible to deny. A number of Orient, East Marion and Greenport citizens had participated in the unloading of the *Artemis* cargo and hidden their personal shares among the brush on the bluff. They were later identified, although not arrested; poison ivy flourished where the liquor had been cached.

No case in the Coast Guard history of the Prohibition era gave quite as much satisfaction to the Base Four personnel as the capture of the *Artemis*. Afterwards, boredom again became a routine part of duty for long stretches; there was little excitement. But, in October, 1931, as inclement weather began to set in upon the coast, some enterprising public-information officer brought his superiors to the belief that the presence of Joan Lowell aboard the cutter *Mojave* would be good for morale.

Joan was a sturdy young woman whose curves fully met the eye. She had written a book, *The Cradle of the Deep*, which had become a best seller and purported to be a recital of her adventurous life aboard a square-rigged ship that her father had sailed as master. It was her allegation that she had a profound interest in the sea and ships and the men who sailed them.

For eight days, dressed in a blue issue jumper and bell-bottomed, tight-fitting trousers that accentuated several of the features of her physique, she was aboard the *Mojave*. While the crew gaped, photographs of her were taken as she "chased rum-runners" and "swabbed decks." She reported her adventures in a series of articles in the *Boston Sunday Advertiser*. Her book, later to be proven a falsification of peculiar imaginative power, was no deterrent to the enthusiasm of the crew of the *Mojave*. They had never before seen such structure aboard an active-duty cutter.

The service of Joan Lowell as a Coast Guard "recruit" was outmatched by only one other incident while Prohibition floundered through the years of corruption and efforts at enforcement. That was the case of the mortgaged rum-runner, and old-time sea lawyers shook their heads over it in bewilderment. The facts were these:

The American-owned freighter *Ansonia*, on the dark of the moon in August, 1927, had tried to come alongside a Staten Island pier with a huge cargo of liquor that was later evaluated at five hundred thousand dollars before bootlegger processing. Police of the St. George precinct sighted the vessel when she was about to put her lines down. They ignored quite a bit of precedent when they reported the presence of the vessel to the Coast Guard.

But the crew of the *Ansonia* cherished the seven thousand cases of whiskey she had aboard. The mooring lines were hauled back aboard and her captain convinced himself that safety for her was out at sea. He ran for it with a Coast Guard cutter from the Stapleton, Staten Island, base in pursuit. The cutter was commanded by Boatswain C. A. Loomis, and in the humid summer night he chased the *Ansonia* hard. Her captain became rattled and his navigation suffered; he grounded the *Ansonia* off Robbins Reef in the Lower Bay. Loomis boarded and singlehanded seized the ship, took the crew in custody.

The case was tried in the United States district court in Brooklyn before Judge Robert A. Inch, by Alexander Pisciotta, assistant United States attorney. On November eighth, after hearing the evidence, the judge reserved decision. He had been presented with a wholly unheralded legal problem.

William A. Nelson, president of the Ansonia Savings Bank of Ansonia, Connecticut, and vice president of the First National Bank in the same town, had entered a claim in court for the ship. He had admitted under the questioning of Mr. Pisciotta that he held all but five shares of the stock of the Ansonia Steamship Corporation, the owners of the vessel. But, he insisted, he was also a creditor, and testified that he held a mortgage to the sum of $39,520 on the *Ansonia* and should get his money back before any government action was taken.

Mr. Pisciotta had succeeded in having the ship's officers arraigned for Prohibition and Tariff Act violations. He now battled to have the government establish its right to libel the vessel. His plea to Judge Inch was that Nelson, through the instrument of the mortgage, was protecting Nelson against Nelson if the ship were seized while engaged in rum-runner activities. He told the court, "If he can produce in this court a mortgage by which he thus protects himself against himself, then I see the proceedings reduced to an absurdity."

It was a real foul-up, the old-time Coast Guard sea lawyers decided. The government would end up getting the ship, mortgage or no mortgage. But, meantime, who the hell did what, and who paid?

A boarding party from the cutter *Seneca* inspect a vessel at sea. *(U.S. Coast Guard Photo)*

The cutter *Seneca* was the Coast Guard's flagship in New York during the early days of the rum war. *(U.S. Coast Guard Photo)*

Coast Guard photograph of a schooner on Rum Row. *(U.S. Coast Guard Photo)*

Crewmen aboard the Coast Guard cutter *Seneca* prepare for the boarding of a suspected rum-runner. *(U.S. Coast Guard Photo)*

75-Footer *CG-262* with seized rum-runner *El Cisco* at San Francisco, California. *(U.S. Coast Guard Photo)*

The destroyer *Downes* chasing a rum-runner. *(U.S. Coast Guard Photo)*

Two 75-footers keeping tabs on a schooner. *(U.S. Coast Guard Photo)*

A New Jersey-based contact boat alongside the Canadian schooner *Catherine M. (U.S. Coast Guard Photo)*.

The cutters *Jackson* and *Antietam* steam into Boston harbor guarding prize catches captured off the Maine coast. *(U.S. Coast Guard Photo)*

Bill McCoy's beloved *Arethusa* returned to Rum Row as the French-flagged *Mistinguette*. She was seized by the Coast Guard in March 1926. *(U.S. Coast Guard Photo)*

The steam yacht *Istar*: the well-known rum-runner was the former yacht *Nahma* owned by New York financier Robert Goelet. The yacht also served with distinction as the USS *Nahma* in the Great War and was a semi-sister ship to the presidential yacht *Mayflower*.

Run Interrupted: A captured contact boat alongside the Coast Guard cutter *Hiram Paulding*. (*U.S. Coast Guard Photo*)

Book Four

THE SHORE

CHAPTER TWELVE

erhaps the most singular fact regarding the gaudy and sometimes tragic years of Prohibition was the American public's eagerness to believe in the authenticity of the various spirituous concoctions they drank. No accurate figures are available as to how much was smuggled into the country, or how much was manufactured and consumed; government estimates clash severely with those published by newspapers, private investigators and those who studied the subject for medical, sociological and historical reasons. But Department of Commerce figures released in 1922, quoted the amount of smuggled liquor for that year as being worth twenty million dollars; for 1923, the amount was thirty million dollars, and for 1924 it was forty million dollars (and in that year a department spokesman admitted that only 5 percent of the total had been seized).

Leading all other items in popularity in areas where it could really be obtained was Scotch whiskey. French brandy followed after that, but seldom received as much attention from the customers; and, as a seller, Cuban and other West Indian rums were a bad third. There was, for some reason, a sense of swank attached to drinking Scotch. It was supposed to be the least adulterated of the bootleg liquors; as a result it maintained the entire market price level and gave the buyer the belief, no matter how ephemeral, that what he purchased might in truth be "right off the boat."

But the residents of the coastal regions, in particular those adjacent to Rum Row, were usually the only people who enjoyed anything like good liquor, with the exception of the rum-runners, the bootleggers themselves and the chosen few permitted to tap government stocks. Many a summer night, the owners of the big estates at Watch Hill and Newport, Rhode Island, along shoreside Long Island, and on down to the Deal and Spring Lake area of New Jersey, kept to their beds while their lawns were cruelly cut to ribbons by the passage of bootlegger trucks.

A landing had been made on the beach, they realized, and their property chosen as a rendezvous for a New York convoy. Gunfire was not unknown on such nights; the Coast Guard, manning the mobile radio units mounted aboard trucks to avoid detection by the bootleggers, had been in contact with the patrol boats at sea. The trucks were light, fast Internationals equipped with outsize tires for passage over the beaches, and the men were well armed and occasionally accompanied by Federal agents or state police. But the majority of the estate owners hoped that the bootleg convoys might escape. That would mean that tomorrow the club would have a good supply of Scotch, and the favorite speakeasies and night clubs in New York a replenishment of brandy that did more than burn the gullet, champagne that was not simply aerated cider reinforced with grain alcohol.

One estate owner in the environs of Saybrook, Connecticut, temporarily impoverished by the stock-market collapse of 1929, listened thoughtfully to the blandishments of a weekend visitor the following spring. The visitor was a handsome, well-spoken young man of Italian-American parentage. The purpose of his call, he said, was to rent the estate owner's Friendship sloop for the summer. He would only use her on a daily basis, return her to her mooring each night and pay a considerable rental. The owner agreed. The visitor then said that he had no training as a yachtsman; was it possible that the owner's daughter could sail with him, show him the fine points of sail trim and tiller work? Again the owner agreed. His daughter passed an enjoyable summer as instructor, and almost every day the Friendship was met just before dusk in the Sound by launches that carried Rum Row loads. These were quickly placed in the broad- beamed Friendship's cabin and afterwards the boat headed back at leisure for the estate mooring. The story, told years later by the daughter, made the young man out to be most attractive. "He had those Rudolph Valentino eyes and he really got to sail the boat quite well."

A freak circumstance caused a scandal and a long-lasting rift that was not healed at the time this book was written. In an Eastern Long Island village during the late twenties, a group of harassed bootleggers, just in from the beach with one thousand cases of Christmas cheer, mistook the spot where arrangements had been made to deposit their burden. They put the cases down in the garage of a house across the lane from the one that had been chosen. The stuff well stowed, the garage doors shut neatly upon it, they rejoined their truck and continued their evasion of the law.

The householder, a local man of affairs, had his elderly father with him for the holidays. His father was both an early riser and a minister of the Fundamentalist Baptist faith. He rose one morning, went downstairs and tried to enter the garage from the house. It was impossible; the door was jammed by whiskey cases. He returned upstairs, awakened his son and announced the discovery he had made. His son should call the police at once, he said.

The son pretended sleepiness. He told the Fundamentalist that he did not understand his words. But the father was tenacious; he tugged his son downstairs for a look through a garage window. The police should be called, he insisted, and the contraband confiscated. There was no use trying to compromise; the son picked up the telephone, although several times in the course of the conversation he broke the connection. When the police realized the purport of his message, they interrupted from their end. But the minister would not stand for any feigning of failure in communication. Unless his son speedily completed the call, he said, he would go on foot to the police, present them with a written report.

The police arrived at last, sorrowful and slow in the execution of their duty. The thousand cases were extracted while neighbors stared helplessly. Triumphant but still watchful, the Fundamentalist rode with the loads to the station house. He was not content until Revenue agents were informed and every case was under government seal.

But the stuff had been counted on as the mainstay of Christmas Day and New Year's Eve parties, not only at the local country club but in many homes. A prominent citizen was quick to state publicly that one hundred cases of it had been allocated to him and that he had already paid for them. He threatened permanent withdrawal of his business from the householder, who was a merchant. Prayer by the Fundamentalist did not help; the outraged citizen kept his word.

Despite the comic undertones in such a village mishap, there were warnings published that should have given the Prohibition drinker serious thought. *The New York Times*, on February 21, 1927, printed an interview with Dr. Matthias Nicoll, head of the New York State Department of Health. Dr. Nicoll was concerned by the increase of deaths due to deleterious liquor. He was quoted as follows: "I venture to give as a cause for this the establishment of a vast machinery for the illicit manufacture and distribution of alcoholic beverages far more poisonous than those generally existing previous to 1920."

A report made public by the Metropolitan Life Insurance Company in the same year said:

"The rising alcoholism death rate in this country since 1920 cannot, in our judgement, be explained by increased consumption of 'hard' liquor as compared with war-time and pre-war-time years. The reason must lie, we think, in the greater toxicity of the alcoholic liquors which are now used so generally throughout the country. The only encouraging feature in this picture is that officials of various states, responsible for the public health, are now stirred by the situation and are preparing measures for its more adequate control."

The responsibility for poisoning the public was mainly that of the bootlegger. He knew very clearly indeed that in most instances, if not all, what he sold was a dangerous product. But behind him were the great syndicates, run by gangsters who felt nothing except contempt for the people who bought what they had to put upon the market. Their sentiment, often expressed, was, let the suckers die, go blind or get paralyzed. Nobody stuck a gun at their heads to make them take a drink.

But in 1930, after a survey of New York's drinking habits, Fiorello H. La Guardia, who proved when he became mayor that his knowledge of the city was almost unparalleled, went on record with the statement that the metropolitan population supported twenty-two thousand speakeasies. He said further that to enforce the Volstead Act the city would need 250,000 policemen, with an extra force of

200,000 to keep the police within the law. The police themselves calculated that there were 32,000 speakeasies, and Maurice Campell, a former chief enforcement officer for the New York district, agreed with them. Grover Whalen, who was at that time the Police Commissioner, described the condition vividly when he said, "All you need is two bottles and a room and you have a speakeasy." Whalen was right, of course; the establishments opened and shut overnight. They often moved from one building to the next or into another neighborhood, and there attracted new customers, were sought after by many of the old. The bootlegger was not to be condemned; he had simply succumbed to enormous public pressure. If he did not sell, the speakeasy proprietor would.

The moral tenor for the nation was set in Washington, where, in the halls of the Capitol and the Senate Building, bootleggers busily solicited trade from the solons. In Chicago, case lots of beer were delivered to the Union League Club at high noon by uniformed police men in their vans. West Halsted Street smelled like a brewery, and in fact was one; practically every building on each side of the street had been taken over for the production of sour mash. In New York, the police made Volstead Act violation arrests at the rate of fifteen thousand a month. During the year from July 1, 1928, to June 30, 1929, the police took into custody 18,589 people; these were for the most part bartenders and waiters from speakeasies, night clubs and restaurants, who were bailed out the next day.

A survey of Manhattan was made by the *New York Telegram* in 1929 for the purpose of finding out just where on the island liquor could be bought. The reporters on the story came back to the city room after some astonishing experiences, and the following facts were printed. Liquor was freely available:

> "… in open saloons, restaurants, night clubs, bars behind a peep-hole, dancing academies, drug stores, delicatessens, cigar stores, confectioneries, soda fountains, behind partitions of shoe-shine parlors, back rooms of barbershops, from hotel bellhops, from hotel day clerks, night clerks, in express offices, in motorcycle delivery agencies, paint stores, malt shops, cider stubes, fruit stands, vegetable markets, taxi drivers, groceries, smoke shops, athletic clubs, grill rooms,

taverns, chophouses, importing firms, tea rooms, moving-van companies, spaghetti houses, boarding-houses, Republican clubs, Democratic clubs, laundries, social clubs, newspapermen's associations."

The liquor smuggled in from Rum Row was only a very small drop in the horrendous sea of shoreside-manufactured liquor, and the original itself was cut, recut, adulterated until it was nearly unrecognizable. The customer who got a bottle or a drink before the land change became too extreme was lucky. Even the backroom liquor maker was callous in his disregard of the stomachs and the futures of those who would imbibe his product. Herbert Asbury, veteran reporter and writer, tells with acerb wit in his book, *The Great Illusion,* a study of Prohibition, of his contact with such an independent operator.

Asbury called the man Tony, because, he said, that was the generic name for all bootleggers. Tony had run a saloon near Borough Hall in downtown Brooklyn before Prohibition. His acumen had warned him that the Drys were going to win; he could see that a case of good whiskey, worth from eighty to over a hundred dollars, would bring him in as much as seventy dollars when cut, and one case of real spirits might be stretched to make five. He invested all of his savings in whiskey and, soon after Prohibition, set up his headquarters in an old brownstone house not far from Borough Hall.

His cutting plant was in the cellar. The first floor was used for storage, and in frugal Italian style, he and his family occupied the other floors. Cutting operations went on after midnight and behind heavily curtained and barred windows. The staff was composed of Tony, his wife, two teen-age sons, a helper, and, for outside work, two relatives who drummed up business and delivered to the customers. Tony held a partnership in a trucking firm; its trucks carried the uncut liquor and the supplies he needed to transform it.

There was little if any noise, and no odors from cooking vats or stills disturbed the neighbors. They were not aware of Tony's business for several years, though they were curious about the trucks that came and went so frequently at night. A relative who worked as a fixer had taken care of the police and the Revenue agents; they stayed away from the place, although Tony had to pay increasingly high tribute to them and to the gangsters who protected his trucks from hijackers.

Tony's equipment was relatively inexpensive, consisting of mixing vats, a tank of sea water and a cask of cider, the last used for an occasional batch of applejack. Then there were tables that held labels and revenue stamps and boxes of multiform corks. Racks were filled with vials that contained creosote, iodine, oil of juniper, oil of bourbon, rye and a number of other flavoring extracts and essences. Barrels, filled to about a third with wood chips, part of them charred, were for the maturing of synthetic whiskey. The stuff was poured into them and sometimes left for as long as a week, was then sold at a high price; it was "aged in the wood." Bottles of all sorts were kept on hand, a number of them of the pinch variety for expensive Scotch.

His "real whiskey" and his raw alcohol were sold to him by a certain gangster syndicate. He maintained a stock of about a dozen cases and several drums of alcohol, refused to purchase from any other source. The gangsters in the syndicate had threatened to bomb his house, kidnap his children unless he dealt with them. Tony knew, however, that part of the alcohol sold him was from a denatured industrial product and the rest distilled from mash in Brooklyn and Long Island by moonshiners who were in the employ of the syndicate. He admitted in answer to a question from Asbury, "Oh, they use sugar, garbage, anything they've got. One shiner I know goes around buying up spoiled potatoes from the farmers. He says they ferment nice and quick. Make an awful nice smell, though."

Tony, as master necromancer, poured the whiskey into the vats himself. At best, it was about fifty percent authentic, the balance already raw alcohol and water. Tony added alcohol to bring the mixture up to proof after the warm water run into the vats had been stirred by one of his sons and the mixture allowed to cool. His standard was approximately 85 proof, even though the label read 100. Color was given to the liquid by the introduction of burnt sugar or caramel. Oil of rye and oil of bourbon lent the necessary flavors, were reasonably beguiling. A bead was produced by glycerine or fusel oil. Tony did not go so far as to use the sulphuric-acid compounds that some cutters added as the final element of their product.

When Tony wished to make Scotch out of the contents of a vat, he put in creosote instead of rye or bourbon oils. This, he was aware, would not soothe the lining of any customer's stomach, but at least Tony had his artistic side, and some of his clientele were quite romantic. They liked Scotch which came in pinch bottles and gave the appearance of Rum Row passage. So iodine was added, and possibly the customer smelled, as he drank, the peat smoke of the glenside pot still in Scotland and congratulated himself that he had liquor with a real bite to it. The customer's desire for delusion was pampered further by dipping the filled bottles in a vat of sea water. These were gradually dried and the labels took on a stained effect; then the bottles were wrapped in burlap in true smuggler style. The extra labor was worth while, for Tony rehearsed his salesmen in stories about mysterious drops from ocean liners, contact boats picking up the stuff and at great risk of life bringing it to shore; the combination of camouflage and fiction raised the price of the pinch-bottle product as much as fifteen dollars a case.

Tony, although ready to deal in almost any kind of alcoholic chicanery, was discreet in his use of iodine. He introduced only a few drops to a quart. But a number of bootleg manufacturers slugged the purchaser with a two-ounce-per-bottle dosage. Others in the trade, when short of the drug or just uncaring, pitched in embalming fluid to ensure potency. This Tony looked upon as bad business, and he had turned down temptation in the form of a relative who was an undertaker and could procure it for him. Tony said, "I knew a guy down on Long Island put some of that stuff in his booze. He lost some good customers. They died."

CHAPTER THIRTEEN

For most of the market, Scotch, whether true or false, was far out of price range. Horrible toll was taken among uncautious drinkers, but slowly, mainly by the loss of custom in the fashion Tony described, bootleggers were forced to sell what was at least not crippling or deadly. The Midwest, except for the Great Lakes enclave which could obtain good spirits from Canada, drank an incredible amount of so-called rye. The South, where moonshining was a traditional profession for many, stayed with the product of the mountain stills, although a great deal of it was "white mule" or sheer rotgut. The Western states, under somewhat the same Rum Row influence that existed on the East Coast, drank adulterated imports when they could get them, otherwise settled for what was on hand and homemade.

The latter was usually Prohibition-quality rye, or, even more often, bourbon. Also, the Italian-American colonies were busy at wine making; Chinatown in San Francisco joined the *Nisei* population and turned out variously potent versions of rice wine. Beer was drunk throughout the nation, needled after brewery manufacture under intermittent government supervision, or created out of syndicate mash supplied to hundreds of thousands of working-class families in Chicago, Detroit, St. Louis, Philadelphia, Boston and New York. These people were really paid employees of huge rings, and opposed to them were the amateurs who had their own home methods.

The amateurs bought mash in whatever quantities they wished in stores that sprang up to supply just such a demand. Bottles and caps were purchased in the same stores. Then the struggle for mastery began while the mash, mixed with water and fervently watched, fermented. The pinnacle of achievement was to cap the bottles when the beer had reached fermentation and was poured. Bottles exploded; caps gone adrift with the violence of the contents scarred ceilings. Floors and walls were lathered and impatient workers gave up in disgust. But the victors had the satisfaction of their own labor. While they drank, they were able to tell themselves that this was the straight stuff, and, boy, was it good.

The stress of the boom-and-bust pace of the times had a deep effect upon East Coast drinking. Beer did not offer enough immediate release for the man who played on margin in the stock market of the late twenties, or, after the collapse, found himself overnight without a job. Gin became a widely popular middle-price intoxicant. In the early Prohibition years, some of the better-known British brands had been smuggled from Rum Row. Their prices proved too high, and the market was limited. Bootleggers began peddling a domestic variety, nameless, reeking of juniper, often fiery and the cause of ghastly hangovers, but to be bought for one, two, never any more than five dollars a fifth.

Mrs. Lucian Cary, wife of the writer and known affectionately as Gus, touched the heart of the matter in the early thirties after a visit with some friends who had left Westport, Connecticut, for New York City. The pair with whom she had visited were artists and, subsequent to the stock market crash of 1929, had entered upon difficulties. Mrs. Cary, aghast, reported their condition in one sentence: "Why, they're so poor they can't even buy gin!"

But countless East Coast people, rather than buy the bottled product from their bootleggers, took up the do-it-yourself tactics of the amateur beer brewers. They purchased alcohol in bulk, a gallon at a time—or, for the more prosperous, five gallons—for prices ranging from five to ten dollars. Then, to taste and expected lasting power, they mixed distilled water with it, put in glycerine to decrease the rough spots, flavored it with oil of juniper, stirred, stored it in jugs or bottles that, for appearance's sake, usually bore British labels, and drank.

The common denominator name for this beverage was bathtub gin. When a five-gallon batch was being made, a bathtub was often used. Social custom demanded that a party be given at the time of concoction, and Saturday nights were favored. The guests joined in with the host and were asked to sample as work progressed. More-juniper, less-glycerine factions formed; guests and host became pretzel-legged in their ardor, lost their sense of proportion, and in many instances the bathtub was left untended while straight alcohol was drunk, the effect cushioned by ginger ale.

Ginger ale was the great, the almost overwhelming concomitant of Prohibition drinking on the Eastern Seaboard. A guest so sick that he could hardly lift his head would save himself from his host's or hostess's wrath by complaining about the quality of the ginger ale, never the gin. Orange juice was the other accepted component for the gin drinker, and in homes as well as speakeasies the Orange Blossom was in constant bloom. Martinis were given a bad name by the specious qualities of the vermouth to be found upon the market; it was almost all counterfeit, raw to the palate and expensive, did little or nothing to disguise the gin used with it.

But some fortunate residents of rural New Jersey, upstate New York and New England were able to purchase, before adulteration, the Prohibition version of the justly famous colonial drink, apple-jack. New Jersey citizens referred to it proudly as "Jersey lightning." It was distilled within that state and elsewhere from fermented apple cider, had considerable resemblance to the Calvados of Normandy, contained both natural bouquet and flavor and could be readily flipped into a Jack Rose cocktail. The price for applejack was around fifteen dollars per gallon, and the supply was steadily depleted. The stuff spoke with undoubted authority, and in the fall seasons, when mixed with sweet cider, was called a "stonewall." After encountering one, staunch imbibers were heard to admit that it hit much harder than Babe Ruth.

But the path of the home drinker was winding in those years, and he was led from it with ease to the speakeasy. There were strong inducements, chief among them food and female compan-ionship. The Volstead Act had put out of business practically every good restaurant in New York City, and inevitably the speakeasies that furnished a menu took their places. Many of them, too, had a twilight atmosphere even in midday, and for the first time in American history women were welcomed at a bar. A lonely man with enough cash in his pocket was sure to discover a female companion who suited him. Then, a number of uptown places deliberately played to the Yale, Princeton and local college trade; dates were made and kept there instead of under the Biltmore clock, and after football games, debts were paid off, celebration routs held, defeats assuaged.

These establishments were far different from the Bowery speakeasies, where the poor stumblebum put his dime on the bar for a drink of "smoke," a frightful and quite lethal product of wood alcohol that had been rectified only by being sieved through old newspapers. Each night after the bums' coins were spent, the gates of Bellevue Hospital on East Twenty-sixth Street were opened for ambulances loaded along the Bowery. The ambulance drivers and hospital orderlies deposited unconscious bodies that were stacked like cordwood before the door of the admission room, there were always a number never admitted to the wards; they were taken in the old green wagon, hauled by a shambling horse, around the corner to the morgue.

North of the Bowery, speakeasies sold a better stock at higher prices. Bleecker Street, in the Italian section, was famous for cozy little restaurants where a fiasco of red wine could be had, and, along with the *caffe' espresso*, a shot glass of *strega* or *grappa*, all of local manufacture. Greenwich Village, east and west of Fifth Avenue and as far up as Fourteenth Street, harbored hundreds of speakeasies. These, over in the Irish neighborhood near the West River docks, were of the stand-up type frequented by longshoremen, sailors and indiscriminate citizens whose preference was a "boilermaker," a slug of synthetic rye chased down by needle beer. The food was ham and cheese and salami sandwiches, an occasional free lunch served during working hours but carefully watched by the barkeeper to prevent the assaults of freeloaders who might eat heartily for the price of one beer, the glass passed with rapidity to as many as three pairs of hands.

It was a curious fact that many of the patrons of the West Side speakeasies, as well as those along the South Street docks and in Brooklyn and Hoboken, occupied a good deal of their time in liquor smuggling. They dealt with the stewards of transatlantic liners who had a few bottles that needed immediate concealment ashore, or corrupt Customs agents who had whole case lots to move, and at night they helped unload the contact boats in from Rum Row. But their personal tastes remained unchanged, and most of the places in which they did their drinking were former saloons, had been familiar to them since childhood. The imported stuff, that was for other people.

In the section of Greenwich Village nearer Fifth Avenue, the scene was much more genteel, although considered by non-residents to be bohemian. Candles burned guttering on the little tables. Murals were on the converted cellar walls, and the drinks served in tea or coffee cups were quite invariably Orange Blossoms. Bootleggers abounded, with gin their main staple, and cordial shops that peddled the ingredients for making the same lined Greenwich Avenue. Don Dickerman winsomely strummed his ukulele in the Blue Horse, the Pirate's Den and the Four Trees, popular resorts of the collegiate crowd, and young couples stepped with care from their tables as they went out on the small floors to dance; "baby," the gin bottle under the girl's coat on the bench in the booth, couldn't be disturbed.

But towards the northern frontier of the Village, speakeasy proprietors insisted upon uptown protocol. Here the patron had to be recognized through a peep hole in a steel door, then passed by a burly waiter who was often a hoodlum with a pistol inside his white jacket. Cards issued by owners were accepted in lieu of visual recognition and a *beau gallant* of the time would carry as many as twenty or thirty of these in his wallet. Princeton men were known to have accused Yale men of swapping them with each other, even buying the cards of places which they had never entered in order to impress their dates.

A very weak trickle of Rum Row liquor flowed into the more expensive of the peephole establishments, and a drink of Scotch might cost a dollar, a drink of brandy a dollar and a half. In the really fancy midtown places, most of them situated in the Fifties, prices were no higher, although a wine card was offered at dinner and reached around twenty dollars for a bottle of dubious Burgundy, fifty dollars for champagne that was even less veritable than its American-made label.

Tony's was a name celebrated by speakeasy proprietors, and

New Yorkers with a desire to impress sometimes took their out-of-town guests to visit the famous place. There, almost every evening, Heywood Broun and Mrs. Dorothy Parker could be seen seated at the same table. They drank Tony's brandy with solemnity and broke long silences with speeches inaudible to the closest listener. The trick was, the visitors learned, to find out if the celebrities really liked the brandy; neither Mrs. Parker nor Mr. Broun had been heard to say as much.

Moriarty's, a former saloon over on Third Avenue, was another speakeasy of renown, but it attracted the sporting crowd rather than the intelligentsia. In summertime the hatbands of the Seventh Regiment and Squadron A of the National Guard were to be noticed on the straw boaters of a majority of the all-male clientele. The Moriarty men discussed the daily double at Belmont, the lack of Yankee pitching talent and the charms of Jeanne Eagels instead of what was being published in the *Nation* or the *Bookman*.

Jack Bleeck's resort for the recognized and thirsty, known to the patronage as The Artists' and Writers' Club and greatly favored by the *Tribune* and *Times* staffs, held long business hours on West Fortieth Street and, in comparison with the establishment of the Moriarty brothers, was considered to be almost effete. Bleeck had a full suit of armor in his place—as decoration, not as protection for his guests. The match game, if not invented on the premises, was in lasting vogue, and among the clientele were artists and writers who worked for the recently founded *New Yorker* magazine.

Near Moriarty's on the East Side there was a walk-up speakeasy that made its revenue quite completely from a roster of homosexuals. The place was as barren as a barn, furnished with no more than a few deal tables and cheap chairs, and the bartender, reputedly heterosexual, morose in his rolled shirt sleeves. The attraction, other than the customers' unanimity of viewpoint, was the Pernods sold for fifty cents per liberal drink.

The strangest speakeasy in New York City, however, was that conducted by the United States government under the aegis of Prohibition Bureau headquarters at Washington. It was opened in the fall of 1925 at 14 East Forty-fourth Street, a fine address and close to that occupied by Delmonico's Restaurant in its dying days. The government place, called by the undercover agents who had rented the premises the Bridge Whist Club, thrived from the opening hour onward. It was, in fact, open at all hours to anybody and rapidly picked up a reputation for the soundness of its liquor, the old-time, homey atmosphere and the generosity of its free lunch.

Trying the oblique approach, the proprietors of the Bridge Whist Club arranged one of the back booths for sound; there were wires leading from beneath a lamp shade to a dictograph in a rear room where stenographers took down all conversations. The idea was to ensnare bootleggers, get them to tell the sources of their wholesale liquor when they became loose-tongued. It worked to the degree that Sam Senate, a bootlegger who dealt in bulk quantities, was recorded as offering a Prohibition agent five thousand dollars to aid him while he brought a cargo of alcohol ashore from a Belgian schooner. But another big-operation bootlegger was too adroit; he sensed that he was sitting in a government web and, although voluble, he did not discuss his own affairs. He described instead the very personal lives of a number of prominent Americans, some of whom were high officials of the Anti-Saloon League, and he told how and precisely what they drank. His statements were never used and were referred to publicly only once, in an article signed by A. Bruce Bielaski and published in the August 13, 1927, issue of *Collier's Weekly*, in which Bielaski, as chief of the Prohibition Bureau's undercover agents, admitted failure.

His staff, even within the lures of the Bridge Whist Club, could not discover who the principal smugglers were. "Our orders for liquor," he said in the Collier's article, "had to be placed through middlemen." The club continued under government management, however, until Congressional ire was aroused by a somewhat different maneuver on the part of the bureau's agents. These men, operating in Washington, had given a dinner for suspected bootleggers at the Hotel Mayflower. The cost of the evening's entertainment for the taxpayer was $279, and the outraged cries of the Wet members of Congress resounded. Further inquiry brought to light the Bridge Whist enterprise and the maintenance of a similar establishment in Norfolk, Virginia, for which the undercover agents had held fervent hopes.

Official government severance from the Bridge Whist Club was announced May 1, 1926, by the Prohibition Bureau. Soon afterwards, the Norfolk speakeasy was closed. The district agents had supplied it with liquor made in stills set up with government money along mule-back trails in the mountain country of Virginia and North Carolina, and had caught local policemen and bootleggers who had connived in peddling the stuff. The bureau's ambitious scheme was also abandoned under legislative pressure. It was fantastic; they proposed to smuggle liquor into the United States and sell the contraband to bootleggers who were then to be arrested. But the Bridge Whist Club stood on stronger ground. The clientele liked the place, and Bielaski said in his *Collier's* article, that it "ran on, apparently undisturbed."

There were, however, government agents both more realistic and more successful than those who had conceived the Canadian import plan. The most active, until fame destroyed their function, were Izzy Einstein and Moe Smith. They came from New York's Lower East Side, and Izzy, an actor by nature, spoke eight languages fluently, enlisted in the Prohibition Bureau in 1920, and soon got his friend, Moe, to join him. The taller of the pair was Moe—five feet two—and he weighed 235 pounds; Izzy, an even five feet, weighed 225, very little of it fat.

Izzy, with arrest after arrest piled behind him, became a hated figure; his photograph was hung up in many speakeasies, underneath it the legend, "Look out for this man!" But he and Moe raided hundreds of speakeasies, stills and breweries, and within the space of less than five years seized liquor worth fifteen million dollars for the government. Their heft was used to wreck huge amounts of distilling equipment, and in Moe's instance, was helpful when they were physically menaced. Neither of them had any liking for firearms; the pair were content to let Moe get them out of trouble with his fists.

They were responsible for 4,392 arrests during their time of service, and though many of their actions had a comic aspect, 95 percent of their cases stood up when tried in court. Figures released by the Prohibition Bureau showed that the pair were to be credited with 20 percent of all the prosecutions within the New York district which were won by the government, due to their sagacity in collecting and presenting evidence, witnesses and testimony.

Throughout, Izzy played the stellar role. He put shamrocks on his coat and, as a loyal Fenian, entered speakeasies favored by Irish-American, ordered a drink, was served, immediately made the arrest. Despite his girth, he passed himself off as a delivery boy; he acted Joe College at Cornell University and was taken as an under-graduate until he moved in upon the campus bootleggers He was in turn a violinist, a dude in full evening dress, a grimy-faced driver of a coal wagon, a lawyer with law books to prove it, and, in concert with Moe, a grave digger. But candor was also his forte; once, upon approaching a heavily locked speakeasy door, he was asked his occupation. Izzy told the bartender behind the peephole not to be silly. He was, he said, smiling, a Prohibition agent. The bartender laughed at that and unlocked the door; inside Izzy arrest-ed him, closed the place tight.

But Izzy and Moe stayed out of Harlem during most of their activities. A white man, no matter what his guise or under what pre-text, was immediately suspect in that area in the twenties and early thirties, and the two agents' recognized the fact. The white people who went to Harlem in those years usually kept to a narrow if not very straight path that began at the Cotton Club.

It was the fashion to end an evening of midtown Manhattan speakeasy drinking "uptown," and the bibulous took taxis to their destination. The gin served at the Cotton Club was no more toxic than the stuff sold in the Fifties; but it was volcanically hot when con-sumed, and had a sweet, heavy odor that in itself could befuddle a consumer's brain. After several rounds, a certain visitor to Harlem left his party one night and went up from the smoke, the clashing voices and vibrant, insistent music to the street.

Lenox Avenue in the hour before dawn soothed him. He felt bet-ter, and in need of another drink. There were wide-open speakeasies along the avenue and he entered the first and asked for a drink. He was served readily enough; still, as he drank, he remarked that he was the only man of his color in the place and the object of some scruti-ny. He paid, departed, and when thirst called again, went into a sec-ond place, where his reception was much the same. He was the only white man, and made conscious of it.

But thirst caught him again some blocks further on and he stepped with reluctance into a third place. There, as he ordered, he saw another white-skinned patron, standing inconspicuously at the rear of the bar. He worked his way around to the man, extended his hand and said, just a bit thickly, "Dr. Livingstone, I presume?" Then he returned to the night and his party at the Cotton Club.

CHAPTER FOURTEEN

Harlem's favorite hot spot was only one of many such places in Manhattan, and each big city supported several. The night club was a new phenomenon in American life, created by Prohibition and still not fully studied by the social historian. The fine restaurants in New York, such as Delmonicos', Jack's, Rector's and Reisenweber's were gone, and the speakeasy which served food was not enough for the free spender who rode the crest of the stock-market boom. He sought the night club, and, nightly, he was fleeced.

The men who ran the big places were the same lot, nearly all of them criminals, who maintained Rum Row. The Row was no more than a fractional part of their operations; the truck convoys from New England, Long Island and New Jersey that came into Manhattan during the dawn hours were dispersed to various garages owned or rented by the syndicates. A staff of handlers, as well as relief drivers, mechanics and hoodlum guards, was at each garage. The stuff was unloaded, distributed by smaller trucks or touring cars to the syndicate-maintained cutting plants. The cut product was then put in warehouses and, when stocks got low, taken to the night clubs the syndicates had established, finally to be set before the customer. Mannie Kessler, one of the country's most daring and successful wholesale bootleggers, had connections with several syndicates, and once delivered to them a Rum Row cargo that, uncut, was worth $850,000, and from which he took enormous profit. But Kessler's dealing was exceptional; the syndicates usually retained rigorous control of their enterprises through each phase, even had their own buyers overseas to make sure the cargoes moved onward to Rum Row.

The syndicate for which Big Bill Dwyer was the front man came to be recognized as quite probably the most powerful. When Jim O'Connell was captured by the Coast Guard on August 13, 1925, he commanded the Frank and Lloyd, a Dwyer-syndicate rum-runner. He was tried and convicted at the Federal Court in Manhattan's old Post Office Building, and the case got a vast amount of newspaper space. When investigation done by the prosecution in his trial brought about the later conviction of Dwyer himself, it was shown that a number of Coast Guardsmen—plus hundreds of policemen and variegated city, state and government officials—were on the syndicate payroll. Thirteen Coast Guardsmen were convicted along with Big Bill; they had helped load contact boats at sea, many times conducted them into port, then given a hand to unload.

Big Bill's outfit had handsome offices which were run in the fashion of a legitimate business, except that there were also special departments other than purchasing, sales, transportation and distribution; these were the political and corruption departments, and Frank Costello was in charge of them. While Dwyer lived high around the town and was reputed to have made forty million dollars out of illegal liquor before his arrest, Frank Costello quietly formed the major decisions for the syndicate, and continued to form them after Dwyer's release from Atlanta.

Thin and saturnine, Costello, his rare emotion shown only by gestures of his bony hands, held such power that in May, 1929, he was able to convoke a meeting in Atlantic City of all the important gang leaders from as far away as Chicago, St. Louis, Cincinnati and Kansas City. The congregation included Frankie Yale and Frankie Marlow, Larry Fay and Owney Madden from New York; Maxie "Boo Boo" Hoff, from Philadelphia; several representatives from the Purple Gang, Detroit; George Remus, whose bootleg rings dominated Cincinnati and St. Louis; Solly "Cutcher-Head-Off" Weissman, from Kansas City; and Al Capone, Chicago. Gang zones of operation were redefined. Tie-ups with subsidiary groups in Louisiana and Florida were confirmed. Then Costello explained to his listeners the logic of not killing each other and not encroaching upon territory beyond their own borders.

The promises made at Atlantic City were soon breached, but Costello had advanced in terms of underworld influence so far as to usurp the rank of Arnold Rothstein, fixer of the 1919 World Series, financier of countless crooked enterprises and part owner of many New York City night clubs, speakeasies and tough clip joints. Rothstein was shot to death on November 5, 1930, in the Park Central Hotel, and with his death Costello's dictates were seldom disputed. Costello had beneath him, in the lower gangster echelons, a muster of grim killers.

Frankie Yale held Brooklyn in fief and was allied with hijacking Vannie Higgins, kept his headquarters at the Harvard Inn on Coney Island. Frankie Marlow had worked for Yale at the Harvard Inn, and also as commodore of Yale's contact boat fleet that ran to Rum Row. In times of stress he was Yale's chief killer and so adept at that work that he accrued quite a fortune and moved to Manhattan. His money bought him shares in some of the fancier night clubs, the Silver Slipper and the Rendezvous among them, and he invested in race horses, gambling houses and the beer business, took over control of the beer sales in Manhattan from Forty-second Street to Harlem. Then, in 1929, Yale, who had gone on some special killing assignments for Capone, was shot to death; Capone had once worked for him as a dishwasher at the Harvard Inn, and this may have been the bond between them. But with Yale dead, Marlow could not look forward to a very healthy future. He had owed Yale a considerable amount of money, forty thousands dollars, and he refused to pay it back to Yale's successor, a quick-fingered gangster known as Little Augie Cafano. His body was discovered in a ditch in Queens in June 1929; it had been the target for a .38-caliber bullet at point-blank range.

But such summary treatment of a night-club proprietor did not deter Dutch Schultz. He was a robust gangster who had made his wealth by beer sales in the Bronx and a partnership in the policy racket there with Alfred J. Hines, a prominent Tammany Hall figure who was sent to prison in 1939 for his transgressions of the law. During the last Prohibition years, Schultz was the owner of the Embassy Club, a lavishly furnished spot which became very popular with the Park Avenue trade. He presented himself at a front table almost every night, and other gangsters enjoyed his hospitality, even spent their own money in the place. The Park Avenue people were variously thrilled; they listened to dark haired Helen Morgan sing as she perched, glass in hand, on the edge of the piano; then Norton Downey let go his sentimental ballads; the Yacht Club boys went through their antics; and out on the floor, customers were able to dance shoulder to shoulder with killers in chromatic suits.

Among the gangsters, although competition was keen, Larry Fay was admitted to be the niftiest dresser. He was a small, sour, evil man who had hit a hundred-to-one shot at Belmont in 1918 and rolled it into a huge fortune. A taxi driver by trade, he took his Belmont winnings and bought more taxis, using them to run liquor across the Canadian border. He also rented and later bought trucks, expanded and worked for a while in conjunction with Big Bill Dwyer's syndicate. But he stayed with the taxi business; his slate-gray cabs, with, oddly, a swastika emblem on the sides, were driven only by men with criminal records, according to police report; it was certain that other drivers stood in fear of them.

Fay's drivers took over the two most lucrative hack stands in New York City–Grand Central and Pennsylvania stations. They concentrated first on Pennsylvania Station; in the long, dark, tunnel-like driveway leading down from the street, known in the trade as "The Hole," many bitter combats were fought with jack handles and tire irons, and the Fay legion emerged as victors.

By 1923, Fay was so much at ease that he went off on a tour of Europe, returned with twelve trunks of London-tailored clothes. He wore shirts of solid colors with them, and ties that made Broadway tourists wince. He was already owner of a number of clip joints, and in 1921, at Eighth Avenue and Fifty-fourth Street, had started the first of his night clubs, a garish dive called Fay's Follies. Some of his old cronies, graduated from the hack-stand ranks, ran the clip joints for him.

These places were patterned after the vile cellar holes in Chicago and Detroit. Standard procedure was a complete lack of mercy for the customer. Pullers-in of powerful build gathered clientele from the street: the uncautious, the careless and the slightly inebriated. A typical joint, known as the Bucket of Blood, was situated in a sub-cellar on West Forty-eighth Street between Eighth and Ninth avenues. The new client found that he had very small chance of leaving it with his cash, his watch, sometimes his overcoat, hat and shoes. The bar was plain and the whiskey terrible; the women at the bar were tawdry whores who would drink nothing except "champagne"—cheap cider or ginger ale. Refuse to buy, and the client was beaten unconscious by the hoodlums who blocked the stairway exit behind him. When he did buy, he spent his last dollar or he was beaten. The New York City Police Department had a spotty record during Prohibition, but when called to a clip joint they were highly efficient. They delighted in breaking the hoodlum strong-arm men's skull's, using the furniture to wreck the bar and its contents.

For his other customers, Fay had a slightly more gradual approach to their money. At Fay's Follies and his later clubs, the El Fey and the Del Fey; at those in which he held a partnership, the Rendezvous, the Silver Slipper, Les Ambassadeurs, the Cotton Club and the Casablanca, he offered in exchange for a whacking big cover charge extremely high prices for low-grade food and liquor, unusual entertainment. At both the El Fey and the Rendezvous, a blonde and raucous woman, Mary Louise Cecelia Guinan—called by her admirers and intimates "Texas"—headed his bill. Texas could not sing at all well, neither could she dance, but she had an unabashed attitude towards the paying guests, and became famous for her salute to them, "Hello, sucker!" She also coined the expressions "butter-and-egg man" and "Give this little girl a great big hand!"

Texas Guinan went on to clubs of her own, but she was harassed by the law, and a number of them were padlocked. She was also a free spender in her own right, and when she died in 1933, she left less than thirty thousand dollars out of her once-considerable fortune. Larry Fay was killed in the same year while standing in front of his Casablanca Club. His bullet-proof vest had unduly bulged a new suit and he had discarded it for the first time in six months. The killers were neat and fast, and Fay was not lamented.

Surviving him was a shrewder gangster who had been his partner in the Silver Slipper and the Cotton Club. This man, Owney Madden, took pleasure in the fact that he was called "Owney the Killer." He was short and brown-haired, with metallic unblinking eyes and a cat-quick walk in which there was always a trace of a strut. Madden came from the Irish-American ghetto of Hell's Kitchen on the West Side of Manhattan, and when he was eighteen, he was the leader of the dreaded Old Gopher Gang. The Gophers' great enemies were the members of the Hudson Duster Gang further to the south, and

Madden reveled in the battles against them. For his part in a murder—
he was suspected by the police of having committed five at the
time—he was sentenced to Sing Sing to serve from ten to twenty
years. But in 1923, he received a pardon from Governor Alfred E.
Smith and returned to his bailiwick.

He found instant employment as a gunman, strong-arm man in
clip joints, bootlegger and hijacker. Probation requirements forced
him to appear at regular intervals at the West Forty-seventh Street station house and report to precinct detectives. He was surly, uncom-
municative about his business, and occasionally the detectives cuffed
him around. He took the treatment in silence, left as soon as he
could to clean the blood from his face and clothing. Then, one hot
August night in 1924, a fusillade of .38-caliber bullets was fired
through the high-arched front window of the station house. Shards
of glass, bits of plaster fell upon the desk lieutenant and the clerical
cop. The lieutenant sprang down from behind the desk and went out
onto the stoop.

Forty-seventh street was filled with people. Parents sat on the
tenement stoops. Young girls and boys played hopscotch on the
sidewalks or racketed up and down on roller skates and scooters.
In the street itself, half a dozen games of stickball were in progress.
But nobody had seen any shots fired or remarked a man who might
have been carrying a weapon. When Madden made his next parole
report, the precinct detectives were affable and brief in their questioning of him. He moved steadily higher through the underworld,
took his fortune from Prohibition, then retired. His police record
contained fifty-seven charges, but except for his earlier conviction
for complicity in a homicide, he had only been proven guilty of a
traffic violation.

But there were gangsters of that era more openly vicious, if less
crafty, than Madden. Joseph P. Loonam, a veteran police inspector
and the commander of the Third Inspection District, which encom-
passed most of the Broadway night club sites in the Volstead Act
years, had a close working knowledge of the city's foremost criminals. On July 13, 1929, he entered the Hotsy Totsy Club, where,
upon the blood-splashed dance floor, two of the very recent owners lay dead. They had been shot down by a fellow gangster, Jack
Diamond, who was jealous of their success and chose murder to put

the place out of business. The execution had been ruthlessly performed while the floor was occupied by scores of dancing couples.

Loonam agreed with the newspaper estimate of a gaunt, wavy-haired young hoodlum named Vincent Coll, who, before his ascendancy to the ownership of the Embassy Club, was one of Dutch Schultz's employees. Rewrite men and copyreaders on the New York City newspapers called him "The Mad Dog Killer," and they were justified. Coll had been in skirmishes with the Jack Diamond mob and had accounted for several of its fastest trigger men.

Coll was a psychopath who murdered with compulsive eagerness. His ego led him to break with Dutch Schultz and he collected around him a mob of hare-brained hoodlums who also loved to kill. Then he started to hijack Schultz's liquor trucks, and with that his life span was drastically shortened. Schultz passed the word throughout the underworld; he would give a fifty-thousand-dollar cash prize to the man who finished off Coll.

The hunt did not last long; gangsters detached themselves from other service, came in from out of town for the job. Coll was marked and must have known it, yet on the night of February 7, 1932, he answered a decoy telephone call from a public phone booth in a drugstore on West Twenty-third Street. His position was vulnerable. Three steps led down from the street level to the drugstore door, which was of double glass panels. The booth was in the rear at the right, the door to that at right angles to the front of the store, and while at the phone Coll could not watch the front door.

One of Schultz's own mob was the winner of the prize. He pushed aside a front-door panel, stood within and took a Thompson submachine gun from under his topcoat. The burst of bullets he fired traced an irregular design along the plywood of the phone-booth wall up, across, down and across again. Coll flopped sideways upon the floor, dead; Schultz's man ran to the street, disappeared into a waiting car.

No gangster killing in Prohibition was more beneficial to the public, and soon after Coll's death, Repeal ended the era. But thirteen years of fumbling enforcement, collusion and widespread corruption left behind them a virus of long duration. It had been easy enough to laugh at the outwardly comic efforts of Izzy and Moe, deride the Prohibition Bureau men who had put a "Closed for One

Year" sign on a giant California redwood tree whose broad girth had accommodated a still used by enterprising moonshiners; thrill to personal contact with gangsters and their molls; and, for the patrons of the Hotsy Totsy Club, witness double murder. The nation had paid much more than fantastically high prices for its liquor, almost all spurious, a great part deleterious and a frightful percentage deadly. It had suffered an unparalleled collapse of moral values, and no brimstone-breathing Dry leader was needed to stress the fact.

The Wickersham Commission, in its investigation of the effects of Prohibition, presented a tremendous number of somber facts. Among them were many arrests of city officials in Chicago and it suburbs for collusion in Volstead Act violations. In South Jacksonville, Florida, the mayor, the chief of police, the president of the city council, the county commissioner and the fire chief were indicted; in St. Louis, a Missouri State Labor Commissioner was sentenced to serve eighteen months in jail and pay a two-thousand-dollar fine; in Pittsburgh, the president of the borough council of Homestead and four councilmen were found guilty; in Philadelphia, a city magistrate was sentenced to six years in prison for accepting $87,993 in liquor-graft bribes; in Edgewater, New Jersey, the mayor, the chief of police, two local detectives, a United States Customs inspector and a New York City police sergeant were proven guilty of conspiracy. And a Detroit grand jury, empanelled in 1929 and serving on into 1930, discovered that the annual tithe rendered by bootleggers and rum-runners came to approximately two million dollars; rum-runners paid the government agents involved—about one hundred of them—29.5 cents a case to smuggle in beer, and $1.87 for a case of whiskey. Coast Guard morale was shattered, would be slow in returning to its splendid pre-Prohibition level.

Rum Row existed to the end and, even after Repeal, although the number of ships was greatly reduced, stayed on to plague the East Coast for some years. Towards the end, nearly every pretense of smuggling good liquor had been abandoned by the syndicates. The ships on Rum Row had become drab floating factories for the manufacture of alcohol. Cheap Cuban sugar was converted in the ships' holds under awful labor and sanitary conditions. The men who handled the distillation were virtual prisoners, the scrapings of the Havana waterfront, and for months-long periods were not allowed ashore. Their product was placed in five-gallon cans for contact-boat transportation, or pumped in bulk aboard small coastal tankers that entered port under various guises and disposed of it with official connivance.

The Coast Guard was forced to maintain the Block Island-Montauk-Cape May patrol, and they encountered savage resistance to arrest. But after the seizure of the tanker *Southern Sword* in the mid-thirties, with a full cargo of alcohol aboard, and several other vessels of her kind, the trade declined and soon stopped. The syndicate leaders had simply decided that greater profits could be made ashore. Prohibition wealth had entrenched them; the system of gang combine was perfected; the underworld, through interlocking directorates or power, spread from coast to coast.

They still persisted. The disclosures made after the notorious Apalachin conference of criminals in November 1957, gave proof of their tenacity and strength. The old Prohibition method of complicity was exposed: the police department of Utica, a major city, was paralyzed by gangster graft; an official bodyguard was provided for the late and evil Albert Anastasia; an investigating commission in New Jersey brought forth that a leading Mafia member, suspected of the murder of anti-Fascist Carlo Tresca, had a direct telephone line from his place of supposed business to the switchboard of the police department of West New York; a number of the Apalachin conferees had pistol permits signed by New York and New Jersey officials who claimed innocence of any laxity in regard to the law.

Paul W. Williams, the United States Attorney for the Southern District of New York, where thousands of Prohibition violation cases had been tried, warned publicly on March 11, 1958, of the danger that confronted the country unless, as he called it, "the Invisible Government" of crime were destroyed. He traced the syndicate rise to power through revenue from prostitution in the pre-World War I period; Prohibition in the twenties and thirties; and gambling and racketeering and other illicit traffic in the forties and fifties. He gave the estimate that in Chicago, from 1945 to 1950, the sum of $150,000,000 a year was played in the policy racket alone and calculated that an equal amount was played in New York City. The Mafia was in the background of all this syndicate activity, he said, and was the connecting link between the factions, the subdivided gangs and mobs.

Darkly seen at the innermost Mafia command post was the figure of Frank Costello. Costello's skull had been grazed by a would-be killer. He was finally enmeshed by the law and sent to prison. Yet he survived, and his wily mind was credited with continued plans for the Mafia and the syndicates; plans to rule them as he had ruled the Big Bill Dwyer regime in the Rum Row years.

The early days of Prohibition had been something of a romp for Bill McCoy. He could not foresee the future. Had he done so, very probably he would have stayed ashore. He wasn't Costello's kind.